Cambridge Latin Course

Unit IVB

Teacher's Handbook

Second edition

For use with British and North American editions

Published by the Press Syndicate of the University of Cambridge
The Pitt Building, Trumpington Street, Cambridge CB2 1RP
40 West 20th Street, New York, NY, 10011–4211, USA
10 Stamford Road, Oakleigh, Melbourne 3166, Australia

© SCAA Enterprises Limited 1973, 1990

First published 1973
Reprinted 1978
Second edition 1990
Reprinted 1994

Printed in Great Britain by Athenæum Press, Newcastle upon Tyne

British Library Cataloguing in Publication Data

Cambridge Latin course.
Unit 4B, Teacher's handbook – 2nd. ed
1. Great Britain. Latin language. Usage
478

ISBN 0 521 31068 7

This book, an outcome of work jointly commissioned by the Schools Council before its closure and the Cambridge School Classics Project, is published under the aegis of SCAA Enterprises Limited, Newcombe House, 45 Notting Hill Gate, London W11 3JB.

CE

Contents

	page
Preface	iv
Introduction	1
STAGE COMMENTARIES (Stages 41–48)	10
The Language Information section	127
Linguistic synopsis of Unit IVB	134
Appendix A Attainment test	136
Appendix B Classified examples of some linguistic features	139
Appendix C Summary of changes from the first edition of the Course	142
Appendix D Words and phrases in checklists of Units I–IVB	143
Bibliography	152

Preface

For help in the preparation of Unit IVB in its revised form, we should like to record our continued indebtedness to members of the Project team, editorial staff of the Cambridge University Press, the Project's Advisory Panel and others who were named and thanked in the Prefaces to previous Handbooks. In addition, we should like to thank, for assistance of various kinds, Pat Bell, Sylvia Duggan, John Hazel, John Henderson, Peter Kesteven, Tim Keyes, Andrew Mayne, Martin Moore, David Stockwell, Jo Wallace-Hadrill and Malcolm Willcock.

The reading material in Unit IVB, unlike that of previous Units, is wholly composed of, or based on, original Latin texts. In the preparation of both the pupil's text and this Handbook, the standard commentaries and other scholarly works listed in the Bibliography have been a continual source of assistance and ideas, and their help is gratefully acknowledged.

A GCSE syllabus designed particularly for pupils who have followed the Cambridge Latin Course is offered by the Midland Examining Group under the title 'Latin (School Classics Project)'. During the period 1991–4, the texts prescribed in this syllabus will be taken from selected Stages in Unit IVB; it is hoped that the contents of the Unit IVB Handbook will be of use to teachers preparing pupils for the examination, and that some parts of the Stage commentaries, such as the 'Suggestions for further work', may provide ideas for possible coursework. Further information about the syllabus, together with specimen papers, may be obtained from the Southern Universities' Joint Board, Cotham Road, Bristol BS6 6DD or any other Board in the Midland Examining Group.

Another GCSE syllabus designed with Cambridge Latin Course pupils in mind is offered by the Northern Examining Association under the title 'Syllabus Latin B'. This syllabus has two features of special interest: to assess competence in the language, a 'momentum' test is set on a passage of unprepared Latin prose for comprehension and translation; and, in the case of one of the two set texts, understanding and appreciation of the literature is examined under 'open-book' conditions, in which candidates have copies of the text (and associated vocabulary) available in the examination room, and are required to answer a correspondingly wider range of questions. Further information and specimen papers are available from the Joint Matriculation Board,

Manchester M15 6EU for those outside the NEA area; for those within the area, from their local CSE Board.

An expanded version of the Language Information section of Unit IVB, entitled 'The Cambridge Latin Grammar', is currently being prepared by the Project for publication. It is designed for students who are starting a sixth-form course after taking GCSE and wish to revise and consolidate their grasp of linguistic points; it would also be suitable for pupils working for GCSE, if they require a fuller treatment of the language than is provided by the Unit IVB Language Information section.

The project has also developed a graded test scheme to accompany the teaching of the Cambridge Latin Course. It consists of a series of non-competitive attainment tests, which are organised on a simple pass/fail basis and can be taken on the completion of each Unit of the Course, with a certificate awarded to those who pass. Tests have so far been produced for Units I, IIA and IIB; further details are available from the Cambridge School Classics Project, 17 Panton Street, Cambridge CB2 1HL.

E. P. Story   Director
R. M. Griffin   Revision Editor
Cambridge School Classics Project

Cambridge 1989

Introduction

Unit IVB is the final Unit of the Course. The reading material consists of selections from a number of Roman authors including Catullus, Ovid, Petronius, Pliny, Tacitus and Virgil, and is supplemented as in previous Units by language notes, manipulation exercises, background material, vocabulary checklists and a Language Information section. The subject-matter of the reading and background material includes the myth of Daedalus and Icarus and its treatment in art, Roman provincial government exemplified by Pliny's Bithynia correspondence, the love-affair of Catullus and Lesbia, the folk-tale of the widow of Ephesus, the eruption of Vesuvius, the murder of Agrippina, and the boat-race in Virgil's *Aeneid* with a translation of Homer's Iliadic chariot-race added for comparison.

The reading material has been selected, arranged in a sequence, occasionally abridged and (in the case of prose texts) adapted, in accordance with a linguistic scheme which continues and develops that of earlier Units. With the introduction of the subjunctive passive forms into the reading material, the presentation of the main morphological features of the language is completed; the reading material also introduces most of the major syntactic points not already met and discussed in the Course, such as conditional clauses, the main uses of the gerund, and jussive and deliberative subjunctives; also practised are a number of other features such as *fīō*, 'poetic' plurals, the use of *-ēre* as a 3rd person plural perfect form, and the interlacing of pairs of noun + adjective phrases in verse.

Teaching methods

Initial reading and comprehension

The basic teaching sequence suggested in Unit I Handbook, pp. 18ff. (reading aloud by teacher, study by pupils, comprehension questions) continues to be appropriate in Unit IVB. But it also remains important that this basic sequence should be frequently varied. For example, if the text is fairly easy, the teacher might read it aloud and pause after each word, phrase or clause for volunteers to supply translation, or might ask pupils to study the next sentence and put up a hand when they can translate it. In dealing with a harder passage, the teacher might first read the text to the class once or twice and give them a few minutes to study it further on their own, and then ask comprehension questions to be answered in writing and marked on the spot by pupils (for examples, see p. 43 of pupil's text, and p. 99 below). One interesting variation is for the teacher to photocopy a page of the pupil's text onto a transparency and display it by means of an overhead projector. This makes it far easier to draw pupils' attention to such features as word order, syntax, morphology, etc. (highlighted if appropriate with coloured pen), and enables pupils to look up vocabulary and language points without losing their place in the text; it significantly increases the pace at which the text can be read.

Reading aloud by the teacher becomes especially important in Unit IVB. The initial reading can help pupils to group the words correctly into phrases and clauses, and can thus steer them away from attempting to translate word by word in linear order. This will be especially important in verse, where the word order may be unfamiliar and pupils may be troubled by a phrase or clause that overruns the line. For example, in lines 3–4 of 'Phaedrus' (p. 30 of pupil's text):

longēque īnferior agnus. tunc fauce improbā
latrō incitātus iūrgiī causam intulit.

a pause after *incitātus* and an absence of pause after *improbā* will help the class to relate the participle correctly to *fauce improbā*. Pupils can sometimes achieve a surprisingly high level of comprehension by ear alone, listening to the teacher's initial reading with their books shut, the meanings of new or crucial words being listed in advance on the blackboard.

The questions printed in the pupil's text are deliberately varied. Some are straightforward comprehension questions; others explore the content of the reading material more deeply, in the way described on pp. 3–4 below. Where both types of question have been appended to a particular text, this is indicated by a division into 'A' and 'B' questions. There is a similar variety in the questions suggested in the Stage commentaries of this Handbook. The inclinations of teachers, the needs of pupils and the time available will all affect teachers' decisions about whether and how to make use of each set of questions, and when to supplement or replace them with their own. One point deserves special emphasis: very simple comprehension questions can often be a means of helping pupils through texts of considerable difficulty (for examples, see pp. 30 and 32 below on 'Catullus' I and 'Catullus' II). Pupils should be increasingly encouraged to support their answer to a comprehension question by quoting the relevant Latin words.

The quantity of vocabulary in some passages may cause problems, especially in verse texts; there is a danger that pupils' initial exploration of the text may be continually interrupted by a search through the glossary for the meanings of new words, unguessable from the context because they are juxtaposed with other equally unfamiliar words. In such cases, it is better to reverse the usual principle that new words should be first met by pupils in a continuous context, and instead preface the reading of the passage with a study of the glossary, reinforcing the pupils' grasp of the new words by encouraging them to recall related Latin words which they have met previously, or to suggest English words derived from those in the glossary.

The reading material is designed to present pupils with a gradual progression of difficulty, but this aim cannot always be consistently realised. For example, it may happen that an otherwise easy poem, suitable for this Unit because of its intrinsic interest, may contain an exceptionally difficult couplet, which cannot be simplified by adaptation as a difficulty in a prose text can, nor eliminated by simple omission. The guiding principle for the teacher is to maintain momentum on first reading, lest the pupils lose sight of the text's content through over-concentration on the linguistic difficulties. Pupils can sometimes be helped by a simpler or more familiar example of the feature that is causing the bother; for example, *nōbīs fugiendum est* might be quoted if pupils are baffled by an impersonal use of the gerundive. Sometimes, however, the simplest solution is for the troublesome phrase or line to be translated by the teacher; then, when the general sense of the whole poem or passage has been securely established, the teacher can return to the difficulty for proper explanation without having disrupted the continuity of the initial reading.

Exploration and discussion

It has been a cardinal principle throughout this Course that the pupils should not only study the reading material from a linguistic point of view but also explore and discuss its content. In Unit IVB, where original Latin texts take the place of 'made-up' Latin, such exploration becomes especially important and rewarding. Often it arises naturally out of straightforward comprehension questions. The teacher might proceed from such questions as 'What did X do at this point and what was Y's response?' to more searching questions about the characters' motives and behaviour and, where appropriate, to further questions such as 'Who do you think was right, X or Y?'

A flexible approach is essential. Teachers will sometimes wish to place the emphasis on linguistic work, sometimes on literary exploration, sometimes even-handedly between the two. It will also be necessary for them to select from the questions printed in the pupil's text and suggested in the Stage commentaries, often replacing and supplementing them with their own, as was suggested on p. 2 above in connection with initial reading and comprehension. Sometimes they will prefer to take time for thorough exploration of a particular poem or passage, and sometimes to push rapidly on. Few things could be more harmful than an attempt to work methodically through every point.

In devising their own questions, teachers have several sources of ideas available to them. Scholars' essays and commentaries that consider the text from a literary point of view often suggest ideas for the teacher to explore with pupils. Balme and Warman's *Aestimanda* blazed a valuable trail in extending this approach to work done in the sixth form and below; textbooks that continue this development include those of Balme and Greenstock, Stace and Jones, Tingay, and Verity (see Bibliography, pp. 156–8 for these and other references). Further ideas and suggestions may be found in the Teacher's Handbooks in the Cambridge Latin Texts series. The journal *Didaskalos* contained numerous articles relevant to the teaching of classical literature, especially in its 1966 issue (volume 2, no. 1). Sharwood Smith 48–61, 87–9 is shrewd and helpful, covers an astonishing amount of ground in a few pages and has a valuable bibliography. Teachers may also find it helpful and interesting to look at some of the textbooks, anthologies and editions of literary works used by English teachers with fourteen- and fifteen-year-olds.

The question 'How would you read this aloud?' can often lead to useful discussion. It introduces pupils in a practical way to considerations of tone by inviting them to consider (for example) whether a Catullus poem is intense or frivolous, or whether a chapter of Tacitus contains any variations in mood. Equally useful is the interpretative question 'What does the writer mean?' For example, the class might be asked 'Study Virgil's phrase *inhorruit unda tenebrīs* and explain what was happening to the sea' or 'Explain the comment attributed by Tacitus to Nero, *illō diē sibi tandem darī imperium*.' Other ways of sharpening the reader's appreciation of a writer's words include exploring the points of correspondence in a simile and examining the literal meaning of a word used metaphorically, through such questions as 'What does Catullus mean when he uses the word *ūror* for his reaction to Lesbia's infidelity? What does *ūror* mean literally? How is "being on fire" an appropriate way to describe his feelings?'

It is also worth exploring the effects which a writer achieves by such figures as alliteration, repetition, assonance, variation of word order and antithesis. For example, Virgil, at one point of his boat-race narrative, postpones the verb's subject to the end of a long sentence, thus raising the tension by telling the reader (or listener) that one boat is in the lead, then continuing to describe the scene before revealing which boat it is; Ovid sometimes uses alliteration to point a climax in his story; Catullus often exploits antithesis to convey the conflict of emotions; Tacitus, at a key moment, uses a long sentence to build up a picture of calm serenity, then shatters the picture with violent action, described in a few terse words. Pupils might be asked 'What is the effect of the alliteration, antithesis, etc.?'; but sometimes it is more profitable to put the question the other way round by asking 'How does Ovid show that this is a crucial moment in the story?' or 'How does Catullus make it plain that his feelings for Lesbia are now very mixed?', thus allowing 'alliteration', 'pairs of contrasted words', etc. to emerge as part of the answer.

While pupils are still feeling their way with a new text, the teacher may often need to use 'leading' questions such as 'What words does Tacitus use to emphasise Nero's terror?' 'Where in the poem does the angry tone give way to sadness?' When the pupils are more confident and experienced, they can be asked more 'open-ended' questions such as 'What impression does Tacitus give of Agrippina in this chapter?' or 'Is there a change of mood at any point of the poem?' Some of these questions may have more than one possible answer; in such cases, teachers should not try to impose their own interpretation or that of an 'authority', but should encourage pupils to offer and defend their own opinions. Pupils should also be free to express their preferences for one poem or passage over another. (This includes the voicing of unfavourable as well as favourable opinion; it does no harm at all for a pupil who dislikes a particular poem or text to say so, and say why.)

Pupils often respond more fully to a literary text if it has some point of contact with their own experiences. They enjoy recognising elements of a familiar situation, and sometimes sympathise closely with the writer or characters in the text. The teacher can do much to help pupils to spot analogies with their own experiences, often through his or her incidental comments (for example, 'The Nicomedians gathered round and watched the flames, just like passers-by stopping to watch when two cars collide'). Direct questions about pupils' personal experiences are rather more hazardous; 'Have *you* ever been in Catullus' situation, Fred?' is unlikely to produce anything but embarrassment. But the teacher can often give the pupils an opportunity to draw on their own experience without explicitly referring to it, through such questions as 'Do you think the thing that really distresses Catullus is the feeling that he's been a fool?'

In exploring a Latin passage, it can be stimulating for teacher and class if another teacher (not necessarily of Latin) joins them and takes part in the discussion. This has several advantages: it exposes the class to another source of adult opinion about the text they are studying; the visiting teacher can give an initial push to the discussion if pupils seem reluctant to volunteer their opinions; and the class are more likely to regard literary discussion as a worthwhile activity if they see two adults taking a serious and committed part in it. Once discussion has got under way and pupils are coming forward with their own ideas, the two teachers should withdraw from active participation and instead co-chair the discussion.

Translation is normally regarded as a means of testing linguistic understanding but it can also be a valuable tool in sharpening pupils' appreciation of the text. The teacher might select a short portion of text (e.g. a passage of Virgil from Stage 47) for intensive study, with class and teacher working together to produce the best possible translation as a corporate effort, written up progressively on the blackboard. It is also useful for the class to look at one or more published translations (see p. 44 of pupil's text for an example), not because a translation can faithfully represent an original but because the teacher can often throw light on the characteristics of the Latin text by asking such questions as 'Which of these translations would give a more accurate idea of Virgil to a reader who didn't know Latin?' This might lead to an attempt by pupils individually to produce their own English versions.

Exploration should reflect the fact that Latin literature was written for reading aloud. It was suggested above that the teacher's reading should play an important part in the pupils' initial encounter with the text, and that the question 'How would you read this aloud?' is a helpful introduction to such considerations as tone and mood, both in poetry and prose. In addition, work on any of the Stages could conclude with a reading of all or part of the text, either by the teacher (in which case pupils might have their books closed), or by members of the class who have each studied and rehearsed their allotted portion; this reading might then be tape-recorded.

After the pupils have had plenty of opportunity to listen to verse, they should be introduced to the idea of syllable-length and practise reading lines aloud (hexameters are probably the most suitable lines for the purpose); for suggestions, see Unit IVA Handbook, p. 39. In due course, they can proceed to the principles of scansion and practise analysing hexameters into feet, but this exercise should be seen as a reinforcement, not a substitute, for reading aloud and listening; awareness of metre comes more through the ear than the eye. Learning occasional portions of Latin verse by heart is particularly helpful for the appreciation of a poem's rhythm; it also follows an important principle of the Course by directing the pupils' attention to phrases and sentences rather than individual words, and it powerfully consolidates their grasp of the language, since it is impossible to learn a passage by heart without understanding its meaning.

Historical and cultural topics

The exploration of historical and cultural topics which has featured prominently in earlier Units should continue here. Such questions as 'How were the provinces governed?' 'How did Roman emperors carry out their work?' and 'How did Romans get divorced and what was their attitude to remarriage?' arise naturally from some of the texts in Unit IVB and are pursued further in the background material. Other texts contain incidental references which can be followed up and explored; for example, Catullus' poem about Egnatius mentions the noisy and emotional scene around the defendant in a lawcourt; the *laudātiō Tūriae* refers to the proscriptions of the second triumvirate; and Virgil's account of the boat-race illustrates the practice of promising the gods a *vōtum* in return for the fulfilment of a prayer. A simple chronological framework for events and authors is provided by two time-charts in Stages 42 and 46.

It is often possible to link a historical or cultural reference in the reading material with what the pupils already know, or to use it as a starting-point for further investigation. The teacher can invite pupils to make deductions ('What is the Emperor's chief concern, judging from his reply to Pliny?') or seek explanations ('Why was the freedman readier than the commander of the praetorian guard to take on the job of killing Agrippina?'). At other times, questions can be more wide-ranging, encouraging pupils to draw on other evidence apart from the text in front of them ('What seems to you to have been the Romans' attitude to the people they conquered?'). Other questions might focus on particular Roman concepts or values ('What do you think the writer means by *fortūna* or *imperium*?' 'Why is Tacitus so scornful of Nero?') and comparisons can be drawn with the modern world; Turia's attitude to her marriage, for example, can be contrasted with modern attitudes.

Adolescent readers, no less than adults, are likely to be interested in personality and prepared to discuss the historical characters who appear in the text. Some of the teacher's questions might aim to elicit a character sketch ('What sort of person does Pliny's mother seem to have been?'); such questions, of course, can equally well be raised about fictitious characters, but when they are asked about real people, they acquire an extra dimension. Pupils can also be invited to comment on the characters' behaviour; Tacitus, with his penetrating and sometimes cynical insight into human psychology, and his habit of supplying two alternative explanations for an action, offers particularly fertile ground for discussing such questions as 'What was Nero's reason for acting like this?' This can lead in turn to the discussion of value judgement ('Was Vespillo right to reject his wife's suggestion?' 'Were Pliny and his mother justified in lingering so long at Misenum?'). It is also educationally valuable for pupils to try to put themselves in the shoes of a historical character and imagine what it would have been like to be in his or her situation; for example, at various points in Stage 41, the class can be asked, 'What would you have done if you had been Pliny? How would you have solved this problem?'

Several of the texts, especially those which narrate historical events, provide opportunities for considering them critically as source material. Tacitus, for example, often offers scope for the question 'How much of this narrative is statement of fact, and how much is opinion?' It could be asked of any historian or orator 'Where do you think he got his information from?' or 'How fair are his comments on this character?' Pupils are often good at detecting bias or special pleading. They are frequently exposed to party political broadcasts and other forms of advertising on television and radio, and are as likely to exhibit scepticism as naivety. A useful exercise is to ask them to write an account of an incident from a standpoint different from that of the writer (for example, 'How would the friend of Pliny's uncle have described the row which he had with Pliny and his mother?').

Consolidation of linguistic points

Consolidation continues to be essential. Regular revision of previous language work not only refreshes the pupil's memory but also indicates to the teacher which points have been forgotten or misunderstood. After a poem or passage has been read, explored and discussed, the teacher will often wish to return briefly to one or two linguistic points and check that they have been understood, practising them further if necessary; pupils will by now be sufficiently familiar with the passage to be able to focus profitably on points of detail. Nouns and adjectives can be selected from the text by the teacher for testing pupils' recognition of case, number and gender; substitution drills and 'question-per-line' work of the kind described in Unit I Handbook (p. 24) can be carried out; parallel examples of language points can be cited and practised. Some suggestions for consolidation are given in the Stage commentaries; collected examples of various linguistic points can be found in the commentary on the Language Information section and in Appendix B. Further consolidation comes, as before, through manipulation exercises, language notes and checklists.

The following ways of consolidating a poem or passage after it has been read may also be helpful on occasion:

1 (Useful if time is short.) The teacher translates the passage aloud, but in order to maintain class alertness and participation sometimes reads

a particular word or phase in Latin and asks the class to supply the translation.

2 Pupils have books closed, and the teacher reads the passage aloud, pausing at times to check (by comprehension questions, or requests for translation of the phrase or sentence that has just been read) that the story is being followed. With an able class, or an easy story, the teacher might sometimes omit a key word from the sentence and ask the class to supply either the missing word or its English translation.

3 A written test can be set on the grammar and/or content of the passage.

Reading Unit IVB on a reduced timetable

Some of the following passages and exercises might be omitted or read quickly by those whose time allowance is short. (When a passage is omitted entirely, the teacher will often need to give the class a brief summary of its content and/or pick out examples of any major new linguistic points for pupils to study.)

Stage 41	'carcer' I and II
Stage 42	'Mārtiālis' II and III; 'Ovidius'; exercise 2
Stage 43	'Tūria' II and III
Stage 44	Parts II and III; exercise 2
Stage 45	Poems III and V
Stage 46	'tremōrēs' II, lines 14–21; 'tenebrae', lines 12–16; exercise 3
Stage 47	'Gyās et Cloanthus' II; 'victor' I; exercise 3
Stage 48	'īnsidiae' II; 'naufragium' II

One way of tackling a passage quickly where time is short is a variation of a method of consolidation suggested above: first the pupils study the glossary, then the teacher translates the whole passage aloud to them, pausing at regular intervals to ask the class to supply the translation of a particular word or phrase. This can be followed by as much consolidation work as time allows, either of language or of content or of both. Alternatively, after the glossary has been studied and the passage read aloud by the teacher, the pupils might answer comprehension questions and the teacher then translate the passage, after which consolidation work could be carried out.

Stage commentaries

Books and articles are normally referred to by the name of their author. For details of title, publisher, etc., see Bibliography, pp. 156–8.

A list of the chief linguistic features introduced and discussed in each Stage is given in the 'Linguistic synopsis of Unit IVB' on pp. 134–5.

The notes on the reading passages normally include some of the following types of material:

1 brief explanatory notes on historical or cultural points referred to in the text;
2 notes and suggestions about possible linguistic difficulties (especially in verse texts);
3 suggestions for exploring the literary and historical content of the text;
4 suggestions for consolidating linguistic points and vocabulary (see next paragraph).

The scale and scope of this Handbook preclude extended comment on the language and content of the texts (for such comment, and for scholarly discussion, teachers are referred to the standard commentaries). The various suggestions for questions and approaches to the text are not intended to be worked through methodically by teacher and class, but to be used as a 'bank' from which teachers can make a selection, supplementing and replacing the Handbook's suggestions with questions and approaches of their own.

The notes on most reading passages include a 'vocabulary check', in which a variable number of words are extracted from the text and listed in the Handbook for teachers to practise (if they wish) with the class after the passage has been read. The class might have their books shut while practising these words, or could have them open so that the context may supply a reminder of each word's meaning. The teacher might also, or alternatively, wish to practise the words immediately *before* the relevant passage is read, to prepare the pupils in advance for their initial encounter with the text. The words selected are almost always words which occur in the Course's checklists (occasionally others are included, such as words which happen to occur frequently within a particular Stage); a few fairly easy words are included, but the 'vocabulary checks' aim especially to practise words which, though common, are easily forgotten or confused. Sometimes an important but troublesome word which occurs in a number of consecutive reading passages is included in the 'vocabulary check' for each passage, so that repetition may assist memorisation. Teachers are of course free to substitute other words of their own choice, or indeed to ignore some or all of the 'vocabulary checks' altogether in favour of their own methods of practising vocabulary with the class. Suggestions are also included, as in previous Units, for consolidating linguistic points.

References to slides are to the Cambridge Latin Course slides sets published with the first edition of the Course. Unit and slide number are indicated; e.g. 'IV.42' refers to slide 42 of the set which accompanied Unit IV in the first edition.

STAGE 41: BĪTHȲNIA

Synopsis

Reading passages	Pliny, *Letters* X.17–20, 37–8, 29–30, 33–4 (adapted)
Background material	provincial government
Language notes	gerund with *ad* *fīō* present subjunctive passive

The five pairs of letters in this selection provide a first-hand picture of Roman provincial government in action. They show some of the problems Pliny had to deal with, the ways in which he tackled them, and the role played by Trajan; they may also give the pupils some impression of both men's personalities.

Title picture

Pliny on his tribunal, dispensing justice.

adventus I (*Letters* X.17a–b)

On Pliny in Bithynia, Sherwin-White's commentary (if the teacher has access to a copy) is full of useful information. Also helpful (and suitable for pupils as well as teachers) are Sherwin-White's *Greece and Rome* article (especially 86–8) and Richardson 74–8.

The 'special status and special job' referred to in the introduction on p. 2 of the pupil's text can be left to emerge from the reading of 'adventus' II.

Notes

(Marginal numbers refer to line numbers.)

7 **excutiō:** a lively metaphor from shaking out a bag. It might be drawn to pupils' attention, to anticipate Trajan's double repetition of it in his reply.

8–9 **multae ... retinentur:** refers to embezzlement of public money by private citizens who had been put in charge of public works (cf. the reference to *cūrātōrēs pūblicōrum operum* in line 12), also perhaps to payments for work not done.

9–10 **quaedam ... impenduntur:** illegal expenditure, such as the giving of presents by communities to individuals.

10–13 **dispice ... agantur:** These lines are taken from a second letter (X.17b) sent off by Pliny when he discovered the need for a *mēnsor*.

11 **mēnsōrem:** A *mēnsor*'s chief tasks were land measurement and quantity surveying (see Dilke, *Roman land surveyors*, especially 15–16). Pliny needs somebody to see whether the buildings have been erected in accordance with the contract, thus uncovering any cases of collusion between the builders and the *cūrātōrēs operum* who employed them.

In this, as in other letters, pupils should be encouraged to interpret the text as a historical document and visualise the reality that it reflects. For example, Pliny's journey can be tracked on the map on p. 2: he crosses the Adriatic and rounds the dangerous southern tip of Greece, then travels over the Aegean to Ephesus, site of the temple of Artemis that was one of the seven wonders of the world (encourage the pupils to contribute such details as these from their own knowledge where possible, to prevent the itinerary becoming a barren list of names); then he switches to carriage, supplied as part of the *cursus pūblicus* which pupils may recall from Unit IIIA (p. 72); suffering from the heat and fever, he pauses to recover at Pergamum (where, appropriately, there was a shrine of Aesculapius, god of healing) and turns back to the sea, probably at Elaea, where the etesian winds which blow steadily from the north from mid-June to September delay him further; his port of disembarkation is probably Cyzicus, from where he travels to Prusa to begin his duties. Since the chief administrative units in the province are the cities, Pliny's governorship takes the form of a continual tour from city to city.

The pupils might be asked in what way the letter's subject-matter changes at line 7. They may be surprised that the personal details about the journey are included in the same letter as the official report.

The picture of prompt and busy activity conveyed in lines 7–14 may be designed by Pliny (as is suggested in question 8 of the pupil's text) to counteract any unfortunate impression made on Trajan by the belatedness of Pliny's arrival; but this interpretation should not be pressed on pupils as the only 'correct' one (they may have alternative explanations of their own). Encourage idiomatic renderings of *ipsō* (line 13).

Slides IV. 42–4 show Ephesus, a carriage and Pergamum.

Vocabulary check: (described above, p. 10): *inde* (line 1); *iter* (2); *coepī* (2); *etiam* (3); *retineō* (5, 9); *spērō* (6); *ratiōnēs* (7); *magis ac magis* (7); *videor* (8); *praetereā* (9); *quīdam* (9); *puto* (10).

adventus II (*Letters* X.18)

The evidence collected by Sherwin-White 536–46 suggests that Trajan took an active part in drafting the replies to Pliny's letters, deciding the point at issue himself and usually dictating the actual wording of the reply to the secretary *ab epistulīs* or other assistant. (Millar 213–28 reaches similar conclusions for imperial correspondence generally.) The reply would then go off to Pliny by the *cursus pūblicus*.

Notes

3 **quī ... mittāris:** This is the first time pupils have met the 2nd person singular form of a passive subjunctive, and its occurrence in a purpose clause with *quī* is likely to cause trouble. Give help initially, if necessary, with a comprehension question such as 'For what purpose has Trajan chosen Pliny?' and discuss the verb form more fully later, when the whole letter has been read.
meī locō: (referred to in question 1) emphasises that Pliny is the emperor's personal representative. Unlike previous governors of Bithynia, he has been personally appointed by the emperor, and his extra *dignitās* is symbolised by his title (*legatus Augusti pro praetore provinciae Ponti et Bithyniae consulari potestate*) and an extra lictor.

5 **tibi ratiōnēs ... sunt excutiendae:** If the gerundive causes trouble, a simpler example may help, e.g. *tibi cēna est paranda* or an intransitive example such as *tibi currendum est.*

7 **eīs ... quae:** first of several examples of *is quī*, etc. in this Stage.
operibus: The drawing on p. 5 of the pupil's text shows an example of Trajan's huge building works in Rome. In the centre of the picture is Trajan's Forum, flanked by colonnades and semi-circular exedrae; on the right is the entrance, the triumphal Arch of Trajan, and facing it the Basilica Ulpia. To the left of the

Basilica is Trajan's Column with libraries on either side, and on the far left the Temple of Trajan. The semi-circular buildings at the top of the picture formed part of Trajan's Markets. See also slide IV.40. Trajan also built the great hexagonal harbour at Ostia (slide IV.41) and another at Centum Cellae, and the *via Traiana* running from Beneventum to Brundisium (slide IV.39).

10 **excutiēs:** Trajan's second repetition of Pliny's verb *excutere*; perhaps he is deliberately, and teasingly, turning Pliny's own phraseology against him to justify the refusal to send a *mēnsor*.

The concern of emperors for their public image could be brought out by asking, as a follow-up to question 2, 'Did it really matter to Trajan what the Bithynians thought about him? If so, why? Would the Bithynians have even known the emperor's name, or known what he looked like?' The latter question might lead to discussion of the emperors' use of the coinage for propaganda purposes (see below, pp. 123–4).

Sherwin-White 527 distinguishes three problems that faced Pliny: a turbulent element in the mass of the population; feuding between members of the governing class; and a financial problem, with which Pliny was especially concerned. Some public money was in private hands, while public funds were being spent illegally (cf. 'adventus' I); inter-city rivalry was leading to wasteful public building (cf. 'aquaeductus' I); private individuals were failing to pay donations which they had promised (cf. Pliny, X.40). Discussion of question 4 might include a second look at the details of Pliny's career (previously met by pupils in Unit IVA, p. 55), especially the two treasury prefectships; do the class think it would have made good sense to send Pliny to govern Britain, or Agricola to Bithynia?

Suggestions for consolidation: predicative dative (line 3; cf. *odiō est*, *auxiliō est*).

Vocabulary check: *cognōscō* (1); *brevis* (2); *ēligō* (3); *ratiōnēs* (5); *vix* (7); *etiam* (7); *fīō* (8); *inveniō* (8); *ideō* (9); *vereor* (9).

carcer I (*Letters* X.19)

Notes

2 **carcerem:** for custody, not punishment. The prisoners are held in the jail of their town until Pliny arrives and holds the assizes.
pūblicōs servōs: owned by the state, as their name suggests. They were employed as clerks and labourers in routine and manual work. Unlike most slaves, they received a (small) wage.

3 **mīlitēs:** Pliny had at his disposal at least two auxiliary cohorts and a coastal force under the *praefectus ōrae Ponticae*. The duties of the small detachment of soldiers specifically assigned to the governor's staff are described by Watson 85f.

7–8 **nam . . . poterunt:** Encourage pupils to read the sentence right through at least twice before attempting to translate or answer comprehension questions.

Discussion will probably be concerned chiefly with the nature of Pliny's problem: Why should he worry about an arrangement that has worked well up to now? (Are the jails particularly congested and difficult to guard at present?) Why does he regard the public slaves as potentially unreliable? From what duties might he be distracting soldiers? (The class may recall examples of jobs from Unit IIIA, p. 93; see also Watson 72–4, 222–31.) What consequences does Pliny fear from possible *neglegentia* (inefficiency? riot? escape?)?

Invite the class to put themselves in Trajan's place and say what they would have done. This is a valuable way of getting them to enter imaginatively into the situation; they can then compare their decision with the one actually made by Trajan. Encourage them to suggest alternative solutions, such as the use of a very limited number of soldiers as supervisors of the *pūblicī servī*.

Suggestions for consolidation: meaning and morphology of *fīō* (3); fear clauses (3–5 and 6–7; cf. 'adventus' II, p. 5, line 9).

Vocabulary check: *cōnsilium* (1 and 6, different meanings); *ūtor* + ablative (3, 4); *vereor* (3, 4); *interim* (5); *accidō* (7).

carcer II (*Letters* X.20)

Pupils might be asked 'What do we learn from this letter, especially line 4, about the way in which Trajan wants Pliny to carry out his duties?' Trajan's concern for discipline might be compared with his instructions to Pliny in 'adventus' II to project an image of a benevolent and paternal emperor; do the class feel Trajan is being inconsistent?

Trajan's concern about the soldiers is probably that the withdrawal of troops for duties of this kind will disrupt training and interfere with more important work; there is no suggestion that it would involve an immediate military risk. The various duties on which detachments of soldiers might be sent, described in Unit IIIA, pp. 93 and 95, and Watson 72–4, 222–31, could be discussed here if not already mentioned in connection with 'carcer' I.

Note how the pupils cope with *ad pugnandum* (line 8); it is the third gerund in this Stage, and the first to be left unglossed. A language note follows.

Suggestions for consolidation: fear clauses (6).

Vocabulary check: *ūtor* + ablative (4); *vereor* (6); *nōs oportet* (6); *pōnō* (7).

First language note (gerund with ad)

For some pupils, who would be merely confused by detailed exploration of the difference between gerund and gerundive, it will be sufficient if the teacher takes them through the examples in paragraphs 2 and 3, checks that they can translate both gerund and gerundive idiomatically, and omits the final question in paragraph 3 or treats it cursorily. Other pupils, on the other hand, will find discussion of the difference between gerund and gerundive helpful and can profitably explore the final question in paragraph 3. It is far better for the pupils to detect and describe the difference themselves, than for the teacher to supply the explanation. The class will usually spot fairly quickly that the gerundive is used with a noun, and can often detect that the two are in agreement. (They can be prompted if necessary by such questions as 'Why does sentence 4 have *īnspiciendās* and not *īnspiciendum*?') The literal translation of the gerundive can be used to elicit the point that the gerundive is passive; but if pupils show signs of confusion over this, it would be better to suspend further exploration for the moment and re-emphasise that, for the purposes of idiomatic translation, gerund and gerundive are generally translated in exactly the same way.

aquaeductus I (*Letters* X.37)

Notes

2 **$\overline{|\text{XXX}|}\overline{\text{CCCXVIII}}$ ... $\overline{\text{CC}}$:** The sums are described as 'considerable but not enormous' by Sherwin-White 614, who compares the cost of the aqueduct at Troas, nearly ten times greater than that of the Nicomedians' first effort. Evidently the second attempt had not proceeded far before being abandoned. Encourage the class to cite any sums they know as a yardstick for comparison, e.g. the property qualification for membership of the *ordō senātōrius* (1,000,000 sesterces) or a legionary's annual pay (1,200).

5 **ipse pervēnī ad fontem:** Pliny's curatorship of the river Tiber in A.D.104–6 had given him practical experience of water engineering, and a number of his letters indicate interest in hydrostatics and mechanical problems generally (cf. his canal proposal in X.41 and his speculations about the cause of a tidal spring in IV.30).

9–10 **lapide quadrātō . . . testāceō opere:** illustrated on p. 11 of pupil's text.

10–11 **agenda erit:** first occurrence of gerundive of obligation with future verb.

Roman engineering skill achieved some famous and impressive aqueducts, especially in the western provinces. (Some pupils will know of the Pont du Gard near Nîmes (slide III.32), and others of the fine aqueduct at Segovia; for a clear and interesting account, suitable for pupils, see Hamey 8–18.) Nevertheless, the Romans sometimes made a hash of aqueducts (cf. *Omnibus* II, 5–6, reprinted in *Omnibus Omnibus* 40–1, for an example), and the hash could be all the greater when inexperienced and incompetent provincials ventured on over-ambitious projects.

Pliny's *mandāta* may have instructed him to refer back to the emperor all proposals for major building schemes. To judge from the correspondence, both Trajan and Pliny were concerned that inter-city rivalry was frequently leading to grandiose and extravagant projects (cf. X.39 for another example: a jerry-built and uncompleted theatre at Nicaea, costing 10,000,000 sesterces). For the prestigiousness of building projects apart from their utility, cf. lines 13–14 of the present letter.

It is worth pursuing Pliny's argument in lines 7–8 to ensure the class grasp the point that water in an open channel unsupported by arches will reach only the lower parts of the city. An alternative method, with which Pliny would certainly have been acquainted, would have been to use a closed pipe, and let the water under pressure find its own level. But without cast iron the Romans lacked the technology for constructing a pipe on the required scale, capable of coping with a huge volume of water under high pressure.

Suggestions for consolidation: present passive infinitive (6, 9, 12); perfect and pluperfect passive (2–3, 3, 7); *id quod* (12); Roman numerals (2, 4; pupils could practise further examples, including some involving the horizontal and vertical bars).

Vocabulary check: *impendō* (1); *videor* (6, 10); *dēbeō* (6); *sīcut* (6); *tantum* (7); *complūrēs* (9); *lapis* (9); *vīlis* (11); *accidō* (12); *dignus* + ablative (14).

aquaeductus II (*Letters* X.38)

Notes

2–3 **medius fidius:** Perhaps mention the derivation of the phrase (from *dius fidius*, a god who witnessed oaths), to avoid confusion with *medius*, 'middle'.

4 **quōrum vitiō:** If help is needed, ask 'What does Trajan want Pliny to find out?'

Some suggested questions

What arrangement does Trajan suspect has been made between the builders and the officials of the Nicomedian council? What has happened to the money (cf. the activities of the *cūrātōrēs operum* in 'adventus' I)?

Does any phrase in the letter seem rather different in tone from the rest? (When pupils have identified *medius fidius*, ask them what they think provoked this little spurt of imperial indignation – the Nicomedians? the grafters? Pliny's naivety?)

Suggest reasons why Trajan is so unhelpful to Pliny over the request for an *aquilex*.

Vocabulary check: *efficiō* (2); *īdem* (3); *ūtor* + ablative (3); *cognōscō* (3, 6); *tantus* (4); *ideō . . . ut* (5); *tot* (5).

supplicium I (*Letters* X.29)

Watson 38–53 is invaluable for this letter and Trajan's reply.

Notes

1 **Semprōnius Caeliānus:** known only from this letter. Evidently he was the local officer in charge of recruitment to the army. **servōs:** Slaves were debarred altogether from both auxiliary forces and legions. Only Roman citizens were allowed to serve in the legions; non-citizens could serve in the *auxilia* if they were free men, and received citizenship on discharge. The slaves referred to here were thus engaged in an illegal attempt to gain freedom and (immediate or eventual) Roman citizenship.

1–2 **duōs servōs . . . ad mē:** Use question 1 in pupil's text to establish the meaning of the sentence, and discuss the agreement of the participle *repertōs* later during consolidation.

2 **mīsit:** Cases involving capital punishment had to be referred to a magistrate with *imperium*.

quōrum: connecting relative in unfamiliar form.
supplicium: Slaves who made a false declaration about their status were liable to the death penalty. But Pliny is unsure about the present status of the slaves (cf. lines 4–5) and seems to think this will affect the kind of sentence (*modus poenae*) they should receive.

4–5 **quamquam ... distribūtī sunt:** The slaves had passed through the selection procedure (*probātiō*) and taken the military oath, but had not yet been posted to their unit or had their names entered on its rolls (for all these processes, see Watson 38–53). Pliny's problem is: have the would-be recruits to be regarded as soldiers now, and if so how does it affect their punishment?

4 **sacrāmentum:** oath of loyalty to the emperor, sworn by the recruit on enlistment. Watson 49–50 gives examples.

Discussion might focus first on the nature of the slaves' offence; see on line 1, *servōs*, above. Pupils might consider why slaves should be willing to run the risk of execution. The benefits (freedom and citizenship) were considerable, and once they were in the army the chances of detection were probably low, since it was likely that they would be posted away from their home area.

The class might go on to consider the legal technicality that bothers Pliny (see on lines 4–5, above): ought the slaves to be regarded as soldiers or not? As with other texts in Stage 41, it is worth asking 'What would you do in Pliny's situation?' Some pupils may reach Trajan's conclusion that there is more than one possible person or group of persons at whose door the blame could be laid.

On enlistment procedures, pupils may recall some details from Unit IIIA (p. 90), which can be supplemented from Watson.

Vocabulary check: *reperiō* (2); *supplicium* (2); *ideō* (3); *nōndum* (4); *dēbeō* (6); *praesertim* (6).

supplicium II (*Letters* X.30)

Notes

3–4 **voluntāriī ... datī:** Whether the Roman army outside Italy relied mainly on conscripts or volunteers is uncertain; but it is clear from this letter that in Bithynia both volunteers and conscripts were enlisted. It was also possible for a conscript to send a substitute in his place, provided that the substitute had the correct status and met the required standards.

4–5 **illī ... ēlēgērunt:** Selection of recruits included a vetting process at the *probātiō*, at which the recruit underwent a medical examination and his legal status was (or should have been) investigated; it is the latter point that concerns Trajan here.

8 **quod:** '(the fact) that ...'

Discussion should be concerned mainly with Trajan's argument. He makes it clear in 7–10 that Pliny should not worry about the technical question of whether the slaves are in the army or not; an offence had been committed at the *probātiō* and all subsequent steps in the enrolment procedure are therefore null and void. The class may feel that Trajan is more acute than Pliny in considering the cause of the mistake and the possible guilt of other people as well as or instead of the slaves. They may also feel that the sentence is excessively harsh; if so, encourage them to suggest explanations, e.g. that the ancient world in general did not set a high value on human life; that slaves were regarded as expendable; that the Romans guarded their citizenship jealously; that strict discipline is essential in an army.

In military matters, as here and in 'carcer', Pliny is relatively inexperienced and needs Trajan's help. However, on financial matters his expertise is greater than Trajan's; hence, as Sherwin-White points out (553), the paucity of letters asking Trajan's advice on the main problem Pliny was sent to deal with – financial mismanagement.

Suggestions for consolidation: indirect question with *num* (2; cf. 'adventus' I, p. 4, line 10) and *utrum ... an* (3; cf. 'carcer' I, p. 6, lines 1–3); gerundive of obligation with verb in future and past tenses (7 and 10; for more examples, see Language Information section, p. 215 of pupil's text); predicative nominative *voluntāriī* and *vicāriī* (3, 4, 5; cf. *servus mortuus prōcubuit*, etc.). The perfect subjunctive passive in lines 3–4 is handled by a gloss and need not be explored at this stage; its next occurrence is in Stage 48, where it is the subject of a language note.

Vocabulary check: *reperiō* (2); *tē oportet* (2); *cognōscō* (2); *supplicium* (2); *videor* (3); *ēligō* (5); *culpa* (5); *nōndum* (8); *patefaciō* (10).

Second language note (fīō)

The teacher may find it convenient to tackle this note piecemeal, concentrating on the morphology and paragraphs 1–2 in one lesson and postponing to a second lesson paragraphs 3–4 and the more difficult (but more important) point about flexibility in translation. If pupils ask about the 1st and 2nd person plural forms of the present tense, confirm that they exist but are extremely rare.

Examples of *fīō* already met in Stage 41 (two more will be met in 'incendium' II, p. 18, lines 2 and 5):

mēnsōrēs ... in proximō fiunt ('adventus' II, p. 5, lines 7–8, used as caption to illustration on p. 5 of pupil's text).
quod ... factum est ('carcer' I, p. 6, lines 2–3).
perīculum ... neglegentiōrēs fīant ('carcer' I, p. 6, lines 6–7).

Further examples:
1 *multa opera in hāc urbe fīunt.*
2 *quid nunc fīet?*
3 *mīlitēs miseriōrēs fīēbant.*
4 *fīliī imperātōris numquam cōnsulēs factī sunt.*

The second example in paragraph 3 is from Suetonius, *Vespasian* 23.

incendium I (*Letters* X.33)

Notes

3 **Gerūsiān:** a civic centre, often organised around a gymnasium, for older men, usually of aristocratic birth and active in politics.

7 **sīpō:** cf. English 'siphon', which works on the same principle. The diagram on p. 17 is intended to show how the pump worked and is not accurate in details. It was a two-stroke action and the plungers were alternately raised and lowered by the rocker-arm. On the left-hand side of the diagram, the plunger (A) is up, creating a vacuum in the cylinder which opens the flap-valve at the bottom of the cylinder. Water is thus drawn into the cylinder, and the valve shuts again when the cylinder is full. On the right-hand side of the diagram, the plunger (B) is down, forcing the water sideways into the central pipe and opening the flap-valve to the outlet pipe. The water is thus pumped out of the outlet under pressure. The same principle is still used in some types of simple pump today.

7–8 **nūllum ... īnstrūmentum:** Equipment at Rome included not only *hamae* (buckets made of rope smeared with pitch) but also *spongiae* (sponges – perhaps for sluicing water over walls near to the fire, as a preventive measure), *centōnēs* (pieces of quilt or blanket soaked in vinegar, to smother small fires), *dolābrae* (pick-axes), *secūrēs* (broad-bladed hatchets), *scālae* (ladders) and *formiōnēs* (mattresses to break the fall of those jumping from upper storeys).

9 **parābuntur:** The tense indicates that no equipment has yet been obtained (Pliny may not have had much time, of course), but Pliny glosses over this by saying he has put matters in hand.

10 **collēgium:** The word can mean either a guild of full-time or part-time craftsmen, as here, or a society of poor men organised around a religious cult, often combining the functions of a dining and burial club. For the political development of these organisations, see p. 23 below, on lines 3–5 of 'incendium' II.

fabrōrum: a corps of civil volunteers (as organised in Italy and in the western, but not eastern, provinces), rather like modern lifeboatmen. The fire brigades in Rome (*vigilēs*), on the other hand, were a branch of the military.

For the danger of fire in ancient cities, cf. Juvenal, *Satires* III.197ff. (making allowance for satirical exaggeration; translation in Massey 17), and for fires at Rome, Tacitus, *Annals* IV.64, VI.45, XV.38ff. (translation in Tingay, *Empire* 84–6). Pupils may know of the great Neronian fire of A.D.64, and might be able to suggest reasons why fires were so frequent. Hardy, in his commentary on *Letters* X.33, suggests height of houses, narrowness of streets and wooden projections from lower storeys.

The division into A and B questions, described on p. 2 above, is here used for the first time. Question B1 suggests that Pliny is discreetly putting forward an alibi to protect himself against any possible blame for failure to deal with the fire. After discussing question B2, pupils might consider Sherwin-White's suggestion (607) that 'perhaps the masses were not sorry to see the palaces of the wealthy burning'. Discussion of B3 and B4 may well overlap. Pupils are likely to say that Pliny's suggestion is obvious common sense, and wonder why he bothers Trajan about it at all. But his hasty assurance of a maximum figure, and his earnest undertakings *nē quis nisi . . . nēve fabrī . . . nec erit difficile* may suggest to them that Pliny is defending himself against anticipated objection. Ask them what they think the objection might be, and see whether they can anticipate Trajan's reply; difficult, but perhaps *nē quis nisi faber* will give them a clue.

Vocabulary check: *dēleō* (3); *opus* (3); *quicquam* (6); *praetereā* (6); *ut* + indicative (9); *puto* (10); *efficiō* (11); *ūtor* + ablative (12).

incendium II (*Letters* X.34)

Notes

3 **factiōnibus:** Trajan's statement is supported by evidence of political feuding, both in other letters of Pliny, e.g. X.58, X.81,

and in the aggressive speeches of Dio Chrysostom, a prominent and controversial figure in Prusa at the time of Pliny's governorship.

5 **hetaeriae:** For the development of a political role by *collēgia*, cf. their possible involvement in the riot between the Pompeiani and Nucerini (Tacitus, *Annals* XIV.17) and the disturbances caused by *collēgia* in Rome at the end of the Republic. For a full account, see Crook 264–8. Pupils may recall from Stage 11 the vigorous part played by trade groups in Pompeian elections and appreciate the danger that professional guilds could develop into pressure groups or political gangs. Pliny had been instructed in his *mandāta* from Trajan to ban *collēgia* in Bithynia, though exceptions were made for the *collēgia tenuiōrum* (poor men's burial-cum-dining clubs). A particular danger was that *collēgia* might attract the professional agitator, hence Pliny's earnest assurance in 'incendium' I, line 11, *ego efficiam nē quis nisi faber . . . admittātur.*

7 **admonendī . . . sunt dominī:** The word order may cause problems. A simpler example may help, e.g. *paranda est cēna.*

8–9 **auxilium . . . est petendum:** Trajan pounces on Pliny's comment in 'incendium' I, lines 5–6, and cunningly uses it to back up his own counter-proposal to Pliny's suggestion.

After the background to Trajan's refusal of Pliny's request has been explored, using some of the information given above on lines 3 and 5, the class might consider question 4 and assess the adequacy of Trajan's reply. Pupils should be encouraged to produce their own ideas, with the teacher intervening only if the discussion seems to be flagging. It is sometimes helpful to divide the class up into small groups to discuss the question among themselves, with a spokesman for each group reporting back to the rest of the class. In support of Trajan's view, it might be felt that a militant *collēgium* could be even more dangerous than a fire, and that private owners might grow careless if they felt the state would always come to their help when needed; also that 'the close building and crowded streets must have made it difficult to bring fire-brigades into action' (Sherwin-White 610). Against Trajan, it might be argued that large and rapidly-spreading fires could be dealt with only by something like Pliny's plan, and that Trajan's advice is not specific enough. Who, for example, is to set about obtaining *ea quae . . . auxiliō esse possint*, and where will the equipment be located? What happens if the *dominī praediōrum* are incapable of extinguishing the flames?

Suggestions for consolidation: gerundive of obligation (7, 9); *is quī* (4, 6; for further examples, see Language Information, first half of paragraph 9 on p. 187 of pupil's text, also pp. 127–8 of this Handbook).

Vocabulary check: *sīcut* (2); *fīō* (2, 5); *nōs oportet* (2); *meminī* (3); *brevis* (5); *comparō* (6); *auxiliō est* (6); *admoneō* (7); *opus est* (8).

Third language note (present subjunctive passive)

The main point to establish from either paragraph 1 or paragraph 2 is that the personal endings of this tense, *-r*, *-ris*, *-tur*, etc., are exactly the same as those met previously in the present and imperfect indicative passive. Pupils can practise the point for themselves by turning examples of the present subjunctive active such as *laudent*, *salūtem*, *dūcāmus*, etc. into the corresponding passive forms *laudentur*, *salūter*, *dūcāmur*, etc. noting the translation of the new form. Use the paradigms in the Language Information section, p. 193 of the pupil's text, to establish that the first conjugation differs from the others in having 'e' where they have 'a', and that the class have met this differentiation already, when they learnt the present subjunctive active forms (Language Information, p. 192). The paradigms of the deponent verbs on p. 198 of the pupil's text should be used to elicit the point that the present subjunctive of these verbs follows the normal rule in having passive endings but active meanings; an example with *cōnentur* is given in the caption to the illustration on p. 18 of the pupil's text.

It is useful practice of syntax to ask why the subjunctive is being used in the various examples in paragraphs 1 and 3.

Manipulation exercises

Exercise 1 Type: classification
Linguistic feature being practised: forms of present and perfect tense

Exercise 2 Type: completion
Missing item: verb
Criterion of choice: sense
Linguistic feature being practised: 1st and 2nd persons plural, present, future and imperfect passive, introduced in Stage 39

Future passive forms of 3rd- and 4th-conjugation verbs are excluded; they will be practised in Stage 42, exercise 2.

Exercise 3 Type: completion
Missing item: clause *or* infinitive phrase
Criterion of choice: sense, based on 'aquaeductus' and 'supplicium'

The background material

For teacher reference, Garnsey and Saller 10–20 is invaluable, and for pupils, Richardson 59–86 and Tingay and Badcock 165–73. There is copious source material in Lewis and Reinhold I.308–78, II.319–418.

The class might begin by studying the map on p. 22. They should quickly notice that the imperial provinces are generally the frontier ones; if the teacher reads them a translation of Tacitus, *Annals* IV.5, it will also become apparent that the emperor's provinces contained the greatest concentration of legions, with *auxilia* used in a supporting role. (Britain, which was not in the empire at the time described by Tacitus, became an imperial province with, at different periods, three or four legions.) Encourage the class to comment on this arrangement (cf. the remark of Dio Cassius, quoted in Lewis and Reinhold II.32, that 'Augustus's real purpose was that the senators should be unarmed and peaceful, while he alone had arms and maintained soldiers').

The map indicates that some provinces, such as Gallia and Hispania, were subdivided, and that some areas were temporarily conquered by Trajan, giving a total number of provinces in excess of the twenty-eight mentioned in Unit IVA, p. 54. Of the ten provinces which could be governed only by ex-consuls, eight (including, for example, Syria and Britannia) were imperial; the two most prestigious senatorial provinces were Africa and Asia, traditionally awarded to the two senior ex-consuls who were willing to accept the governorship and had not previously held it. (Coincidentally, the two leading historical characters in the pupil's earlier reading material, Agricola and Salvius, both at different times turned down the governorship of Asia; for Agricola's refusal, cf. Tacitus, *Agricola* 42.)

A selection from the following points may be useful in supplementing the pupil's material (the sub-headings follow roughly the order in which information is presented in the pupil's text). Encourage pupils to recall points they have met earlier in the Course, in either the reading passages or the background material, that illustrate or link with the present topic. Where time allows, it is valuable for pupils to ferret out some of the information from their own researches, working in small groups and using either such handbooks as Richardson or (under the teacher's guidance) translations of primary sources, e.g. in Lewis and Reinhold.

Length of governorship. Governorship of a senatorial province was normally for one year. Governorship of an imperial province usually lasted for three years, but could run for longer; for example, Agricola governed Britain for seven years, and Poppaeus Sabinus (grandfather of Poppaea, the *femme fatale* of Stage 48) was kept in his post by Tiberius for twenty-four.

Special expertise of Agricola and Pliny. The careers of both men were given in Unit IVA, p. 55. Encourage pupils to recall that Pliny served in two treasury posts and Agricola had experience of Britain both as military tribune and as legionary commander before going there as governor.

Saint Paul. For Paul's trials before two Roman governors, Felix and Festus, see *Acts* 24–5, and for his adventures en route for Rome, *Acts* 27–8.

Position of 'iūridicus'. A *iūridicus* was subordinate to the governor. The pupils have met a fictionalised presentation of a clash between governor and *iūridicus* in Unit IIIA, p. 104, where Agricola claims *summa potestās* (and legally is in the right) but his *iūridicus* Salvius has more power in reality, since he enjoys more of the emperor's confidence.

Unsuccessful building projects. Slide IV.50 shows the remains of one such project, the botched vaulting of the theatre at Nicaea, about which Pliny writes in X.39.

The final quotations are from Tacitus, *Agricola* 21 and 30.

Mention might be made of the Romans' use of client-kings and buffer-states, as alternatives to taking territory over as a province. Sometimes a native ruler, such as Cogidubnus among the Regnenses in Britain, and Herod in Judaea, became a 'client-king' and enjoyed a measure of independence in governing his people, provided he did not act against Rome's interests; at other times, a treaty of friendship might be concluded with a friendly 'buffer-state' such as Armenia, who received Roman support against more dangerous neighbours.

The drawing based on the Peutinger Table (pp. 24–5 of the pupil's text) is the sort of map that might have been available for Pliny to use. Pupils may be interested to compare it with the modern map on p. 2. The Peutinger Table is a medieval copy of an itinerary of the Roman empire, in pictorial form – a diagram rather than a map, for there is considerable distortion in the drawing of geographical features. It is intended to show the cities and post stages touched by the major roads and the distances between them. Fixed symbols are used to indicate the sizes of the towns and the facilities available in them. As in a modern motoring guide, a reasonable inn, for example, is indicated by a house with a twin-peaked roof and very basic accommodation by a single house. For further details see Casson 186–8 and Dilke, *Greek and Roman maps* 112–20 and 193–5. The original may have been compiled in the fourth century, perhaps on a basis of older works. The Table is a parchment roll in Vienna, but there is a facsimile in the Museum of Classical Archaeology, Cambridge. (Part of this facsimile is shown on slide IV.45.)

The photograph on p. 26 of the pupil's text shows a messenger travelling by the *cursus pūblicus* (described in Unit IIIA, p. 72). Pliny puts various queries to Trajan (e.g. X.45, X.64, X.120) about the correct use of the *cursus pūblicus* and the issuing of official passes (*diplōmata*) to would-be travellers.

Suggestions for discussion

1 When Tiberius' advisers suggested he should squeeze all the money he could from the provinces by taxation, he replied (Suetonius, *Tiberius* 32) 'A good shepherd shears his sheep; he doesn't skin them.' What did he mean by this? Was he being kind or calculating?

2 Suggest reasons why a king might deliberately choose to bequeath his kingdom to the Romans.

3 Why did such an important province as Egypt have only an equestrian governor? (To emphasise that Egypt was a politically sensitive province, the teacher might add that no senator was allowed even to visit it without special permission. The class may recall Rome's heavy dependence on Egyptian corn, and some pupils may have heard of Antony and Cleopatra's use of Egypt as a base in the civil war with Augustus.)

4 Augustus, in his will (Tacitus, *Annals* I.11), advised his successors not to enlarge the empire beyond its existing size. Suggest reasons, either creditable or otherwise, why he gave this advice. (Tacitus' suggestions are *metus* and *invidia*. Claudius' invasion of Britain was the only important instance of disregard of Augustus' advice until the time of Trajan.)

5 How justified is Tacitus' cynical comment (*Agricola* 21, quoted on p. 27 of pupil's text) that the trappings of Roman civilisation, such as colonnades and baths, were in reality part of the Britons' slavery?

6 Compare Calgacus' attack on Roman imperialism (Tacitus, *Agricola* 30–2) with the defence made by Cerialis (Tacitus, *Histories* IV.73–4).

Vocabulary checklist

Pupils are likely to need help with the checklists in this Unit, which contain some words met only once or twice in the Course. Some of the words in the checklist should be discussed before it is set for homework; for example, the teacher might remind the class of the contexts where they met *iūs* ('incendium' I, p. 16, line 12) and *opus est* ('aquaeductus' I, p. 10, line 4; 'incendium' II, p. 18, line 8), and the two different ways of translating *nec* could be practised.

Some cognate words, both new and familiar, are added at the end of each checklist in this Unit, to practise the principles of word-formation and remind the pupils that if they know the meaning of a given word they will often find it helps them to cope with several other related words. If a particular suffix causes trouble (e.g. *-tās* in *vīlitās*), remind the class of some simpler or more familiar examples (*crūdēlitās* from *crūdēlis*, *tranquillitās* from *tranquillus*, etc.).

Suggestions for further work

1 Ask the class to describe one of the situations in Stage 41 through the eyes of a newspaper reporter. Encourage them to supplement narrative and reported interview with editorial comment, and to devise headlines which reflect the writer's sympathies ('Pliny Intervenes over Slave Scandal' or 'Public Uproar at Veto of Fire Safety Plan'). If the class has access to a suitable translation, this exercise could be extended to other letters in Book X, in addition to those included in Stage 41.

2 The class could consider the much-discussed question of Pliny's competence as a governor. Does his correspondence indicate efficiency or fussiness, conscientiousness or lack of initiative? Which of the letters in Stage 41, if any, strike the pupils as unnecessary (cf. Sherwin-White 546–55)?

3 Pupils might be asked to compose a letter, supposedly by Pliny to a friend, in which he describes either his life in Bithynia or one of the Stage 41 situations more informally and frankly than in his letters to Trajan.

STAGE 42: CARMINA

Synopsis

Reading passages	Phaedrus, *Fables* I.1 Catullus, *Poems* 39 and 101 Martial, *Epigrams* IV.69; VII.83; X.8 Ovid, *Ars Amatoria* I.469–78 Virgil, *Aeneid* III.192–206
Background material	time-chart (poets and historical events)
Language notes	conditional clauses verse word order: interlacing of noun + adjective phrases

The reading passages in this Stage have been chosen as short but characteristic samples of the work of a number of different poets in a wide variety of genres including fable, elegy, epigram, didactic (parodied) and epic.

Title picture

Virgil composing the *Aeneid* (based on a mosaic from Tunisia). The scroll bears the invocation to the Muse, *musa, mihi causas memora, quo numine laeso quidve* . . . (*Aeneid* I.8–9).

Phaedrus (*Fables* I.1)

Notes

2–3 **superior . . . īnferior:** predicative; cf. *mortuus prōcubuit, immōtī adstābant*, etc.
3–4 **fauce improbā . . . incitātus:** See p. 2 above.
13 **iniūstā nece:** Discuss with the class the best way of translating the ablative here.

The questions printed in the pupil's text in this Stage vary in type from author to author; some are easy comprehension questions, to aid as well as test understanding, while others are more probing, to encourage literary exploration after the surface meaning has been established. Those on Phaedrus are fairly straightforward; if the teacher wishes to give extra help they can be further simplified, e.g.:

What two animals appear in line 1?
What had they done (refer class to the picture if necessary)? Why had they come?
What was the wolf doing? etc.

Agreement of separated noun and adjective is indicated from time to time in this Unit by underlining, as in lines 5–6. As the pupils' experience of reading verse increases, this use of underlining is steadily reduced during the course of the Unit, though it continues to be employed in cases of difficulty.

After using question 6 to establish Phaedrus' moral ('Might is right', 'Jungle law', 'Any excuse will do', etc.), the teacher could ask the class whether it is an accurate comment on human nature.

Suggestions for consolidation: present participle (6); 2nd person singular present deponent (7); perfect passive participle in nominative (2, 4, 9) and accusative (13; cf. Stage 41, p. 12, line 2).

Vocabulary check: *īdem* (1); *longē* (3); *incitō* (4); *quārē* (5); *queror* (7).

Catullus I (from *Poem* 39)

Commentaries: Fordyce, Quinn.

If the reading of the text is preceded by study of the glossary (see pp. 2–3), the words in the glossary should in at least some cases be discussed, not merely looked at. For example, *candidus* can be linked with *candidātus*, *ōrātor* with *ōrāre*; the connection between the glosses on *urbānus* in lines 8 and 10 can be explored, and compared with the meanings of *rūsticus*; other examples of impersonal passives (e.g. *curritur*, *clāmātur*, *venitur*) can be added to *lūgētur* and *ventum est*.

Notes

2–4 **sī . . . ille:** The prisoner's friends sit near him in court to give moral and vocal support. The picture on p. 33 shows the scene, with the pleader appealing to the audience's emotions in a *miserātiō*, while the defendant's wife and family add to the pathos. Encourage the class to identify Egnatius in the picture.

4 **ad:** the meaning ('at') may have been forgotten, but is included in the wording of pupil's question 2.

5 **orba cum flet:** *cum* postponed from 'normal' position. The pupil's text sometimes gives help with such postponements in Unit IVB, either by underlining words on either side of the postponed word or by including a note in the glossary. The teacher should also remind the pupils to read the phrase or sentence right through before translating.

7 **morbum:** predicative accusative. Encourage such renderings as 'this is a disease he has'.

9 **monendum est tē:** unusual and difficult variation on *monendus es*.

If the questions in the pupil's text need to be simplified, the following may help:

What does Egnatius possess? And what does he therefore do?
Where does Catullus imagine Egnatius has arrived (refer pupils to the picture if necessary)? What is going on there? What does Egnatius do?
What activity does Catullus then imagine is taking place? Where? Who is present? What is she doing? etc.

Question 2 can be further extended; encourage the class to pick out and comment on such words as *piī* and *ūnicum*, which stress the mournfulness of the occasion and therefore the inappropriateness of Egnatius' behaviour.

Some pupils habitually reply to such questions as no. 3 by saying 'for emphasis'; they should be pressed to say what is being emphasised. It might be noted that the repetitions of *renīdet* nearly all occur at the same point of the line, highlighting the maddeningly predictable repetition of Egnatius' smirk.

The class could be asked 'How does Catullus stop the list of names in lines 10–11 from becoming monotonous?' When they have grasped the function of the adjectives, they could be invited to devise modern analogies ('If you were a kilted Scotsman' etc.), provided this can be done without ruffling regional sensitivities of individuals in the class.

If the teacher asks the class 'How do we know what Catullus wrote?' their replies usually reveal that they naturally but wrongly believe that Catullus' autograph MS. survives, and they are amazed to learn that the oldest surviving MSS. of Catullus were written fourteen centuries after the poet's death. The variant readings in line 11, *pinguis* (from a grammarian's quotation) and *parcus* (MSS. reading) might be mentioned: which reading appeals more to the pupils? The purpose of such discussion is not to train the pupils as textual critics but to introduce the idea that the words of Roman writers are not known as certainties but have to be reconstructed by the labours of scholars. On the copying of an author's work, cf. Unit IVA, p. 96; and see Tingay and Badcock 153–5, and Dilke, *Ancient Romans* 165–7.

The implication that Egnatius' methods of dental hygiene are in some way unsavoury is conveyed in lines 10–12, and it is hoped that question 6 will bring this out. At the teacher's discretion, the class might then study the final lines of the poem, written up on the blackboard, in which the details of Egnatius' habit are revealed with cheerful coarseness:

nunc Celtiber es: Celtiberia in terra,
quod quisque minxit, hoc sibi solet mane
dentem atque russam defricare gingivam
ut, quo iste vester expolitior dens est,
hoc te amplius bibisse praedicet loti.

Suggestions for consolidation: ablative of comparison (14).

Vocabulary check: *ut* + indicative (8).

Catullus II (*Poem* 101)

Commentaries: Fordyce, Quinn.

Notes

2 **ad:** meaning 'at' or 'for' (cf. 'Catullus' I, p. 32, line 4) recurs in line 8.
īnferiās: an offering to the *dī mānēs*, consisting of wine, milk, honey and flowers, illustrated in pupil's text.

6 **adēmpte:** The case often causes trouble. If pupils translate as 'You have been taken away', point out that there is no *es*.

7–9 **haec ... accipe ... mānantia:** This is where the pupils will probably need most help. With the aid of the footnote in the text, guide them to take *haec* as the object of *accipe*, qualified by *mānantia*.

9 **mānantia:** The idea may seem bizarre and exaggerated to pupils; encourage them to see it as normal behaviour in a first-century Roman context.

The questions in the pupil's text are intended for a late stage in the reading of the poem, after the surface meaning has been established. Easier questions to assist the initial reading might begin with such questions as these:

What has happened to Catullus' brother? Did it happen in Rome? Near Rome?
Was Catullus there?
Where is Catullus now? What ceremony has he come for?
What is he going to do? What else (line 4)?

When the surface meaning of the text has been established, the class might be asked to outline the situation depicted in the poem, with the teacher supplying additional data where needed. Catullus' brother has died in the Troad, and Catullus, probably en route in 57 B.C. to the province of Bithynia, where he was on the governor's staff, has paid a visit to the resting-place of his brother's ashes, bringing the traditional offerings to the dead; he laments his brother and utters the formal farewell *avē atque valē*. The ceremony has a special poignancy, since it takes place far from home and Catullus is the sole mourner. It is often misinterpreted by pupils as a funeral; guide them to a better analogy, e.g. putting flowers on a grave. Part of the ceremony (the utterance of *avē atque valē*) is incorporated into the poem, so that the poem both enacts Catullus' performance of the ritual and includes what could be taken as his spoken or unspoken thoughts as he performs it (see Quinn, *LE* 80ff.).

Question 2 can be considered briefly at an early stage of discussion (and answered simply, 'To visit his brother's grave') and reconsidered more thoroughly later ('Has he come because he wants to, or because he thinks he ought to? Does he think his visit will do himself or his brother any good? Does he "believe" in the ritual?').

Question 4 might lead to the apparent contradiction of *intereā* (line 7) and *in perpetuum* (line 10). Even if this is resolved by following the commentators who interpret *intereā* as 'in the circumstances, as things are', inconsistencies seem to remain. If Catullus' brother can hear him now, why does he talk in line 10 of a final separation? If he doesn't believe in an afterlife, why does he speak to his brother and why does he bring the offerings and stress them so prominently in the poem? If there *is* inconsistency, does it weaken or strengthen the poem's effectiveness?

Other points for exploration include the meaning of *mūnere mortis* in line 3 (see Lyne, *Handbook* 56 for a valuable discussion of this and other points) and the significance of *indigne* in line 6 ('All men die; why is the death of Catullus' brother "unfair"?').

The poem provides a good opportunity for studying assonance and alliteration. Read it aloud to the class and invite comment on its sound. From listening or looking, they are likely to pick up the high incidence of 'm' (23 of the poem's 63 words contain 'm', 13 in initial position) and may notice other instances of verbal patterning, e.g. with the letter 'f'. Do they think this is coincidence or design? What is the effect? If they feel that the assonance and alliteration intensify the mournful dirge-like tone of the poem, do they think this is because the sound of 'm' is peculiarly melancholy or because the assonance and alliteration, like salt in food, highlight an element already present? (See Wilkinson 25ff. for the view that usually sound is expressive only when it reinforces meaning.)

Balme and Warman 44–5 quote two translations of this poem for comparison.

The imperfect subjunctive deponent *adloquerer* (line 4) and the dative of disadvantage *mihī* (line 5) are handled by glosses, and there is no need to explore them further at this stage. They are the subject of language notes in Stages 43 and 45 respectively.

Vocabulary check: *gēns* (1); *cinis* (4); *auferō* (5); *mōs* (7).

Mārtiālis I (*Epigrams* IV.69)

The word order in line 3, and the case of *hāc lagōnā*, may cause trouble. Ask the class 'What is said to have happened to Papylus? How?' The point of the epigram, if pupils do not see it, can be elicited by asking 'Does Martial at any point admit to believing the rumours about Papylus? What does the poem suggest about his real opinion?'

The relief on p. 36 of the pupil's text, showing slaves filling goblets from assorted jugs and jars, is from the third-century funerary Igel Monument, from near Trier.

Suggestions for consolidation: present, future and imperfect indicative passive and deponent endings (3; cf. *quereris* in 'Phaedrus', p. 30, line 7, *arbitror* in 'Catullus' I, p. 32, line 8, *afflīgēbar*, *ūtar*, *verēris* and *suspicor* in Stage 41 and the *-mur*, *-minī* endings in Stage 41 exercise 2, and for further practice the Language Information section of the pupil's text, p. 190, paragraph 2, and p. 196, paragraphs 2 and 3).

Vocabulary check: *vel* (1); *negō* (2); *fīō* (3); *puto* (4).

Mārtiālis II (*Epigrams* VII.83)

For commentary, see Tennick 72. He notes the literal meaning of the Greek name Eutrapelus ('Dexterous', 'Nimble-fingers'), and the use of rouge after shaving (*expingit*, line 2), then raises the question of Martial's target: is he satirising the slowness and finickiness of Eutrapelus, or the hairiness of Lupercus (cf. *lupus*)?

Vocabulary check: *dum* (1); *ōs* (1).

Mārtiālis III (*Epigrams* X.8)

Note the two different verbs meaning 'marry': *dūcō* ('I take a wife') and *nūbō* ('I put on the marriage veil'), depending on whether the groom or bride is the subject; the distinction faithfully reflects a Roman attitude to marriage.

Vocabulary check: *nūbō* (1); *cupiō* (1); *magis* (2).

It is sometimes helpful to ask the class 'If Martial were alive today, for which television programme do you think he would be a scriptwriter?'

Pupils might be asked to produce a written verse translation of one of the three Martial epigrams in this Stage. Free verse will probably be more effective than a rigid rhyme-and-metre scheme. The aim should be to retain the brevity of the original and reserve the climax of the epigram until the final word or phrase.

First language note (conditional clauses)

For further practice, examples of conditional clauses from earlier in the Unit can be picked out and retranslated. For instance:

sī tū dīligenter excutiēs, inveniēs. (Stage 41, p. 5, line 10)
sī quid adversī . . ., poterunt. (Stage 41, p. 6, lines 7–8)
sī mīlitēs . . ., rēctē verēris . . . (Stage 41, p. 7, lines 5–6)
sī lēctī sunt, . . . pūniendī erunt. (Stage 41, p. 13, lines 4–7)
sī ad reī . . ., renīdet ille; sī ad piī . . . renīdet ille. ('Catullus' I, p. 32, lines 2–6)

When taking the class through the examples in paragraph 4, practise both ways of translating *nisi*.

Paragraph 5 makes a deliberately brief mention of subjunctive conditional sentences, of which only two examples have occurred in the Unit so far. Concentrate on the correspondence between the use of the subjunctive in the Latin sentence and the translation 'would' or 'should' in the English, and do not at this stage analyse the use of the different tenses. The commonest type of subjunctive conditional sentence, involving the pluperfect subjunctive in both main clause and conditional clause, is the subject of a language note in Stage 46.

For an entertaining ghost story in which Latin lessons and conditional clauses play a prominent part, see 'A School Story' in James 7–15.

Ovidius (*Ars Amatoria* I.469–78)

Commentary: Hollis.

Notes

4 **equī:** delayed subject. Remind the class of the importance of reading the line right through, and use comprehension questions such as 'What are the next animals to be mentioned? What does Ovid say about them?'

6 **assiduā . . . humō:** Stress the need to make the sense clear in translation, and encourage pupils to reject 'continual ground' in favour of 'continual contact with the ground', etc.

9 **perstā modo:** The parenthesis separates the object from the verb; careful phrasing and intonation when reading aloud will help.

The questions in the pupil's text are intended for use after the passage has been read and translated and the surface meaning understood. The class might be invited to summarise Ovid's advice as briefly as possible (can they boil it down to three words?) or to cite any proverbs or anecdotes that convey the same advice as Ovid ('If at first you don't succeed . . .', 'Remember Bruce and the spider', etc.). Pupils could also be asked 'Which is the key word in Ovid's argument?' (point them to lines 3, 4 and 10 if necessary) and 'Find a word in lines 5–6, not necessarily a noun, that conveys the same idea as the key word.'

The final part of question 1 may provoke the class to contrast the logic (or lack of it) in Ovid's argument with its psychological effectiveness. To say 'Other people have succeeded; therefore so will you' is strictly a non-sequitur, but may still be a good way of raising morale.

Ovid has also a literary reason for his use of *exempla* in these lines: such *exempla* are typical features of didactic poetry, which Ovid is here parodying. The point could be demonstrated by reading the class a translation of some didactic verse, e.g. Lucretius I.311ff., quoted by Balme and Warman 34–5, and asking pupils to compare it with Ovid. Ovid and Lucretius both use *exempla* (sometimes the same ones) to make their point, but in Lucretius tone and theme are serious, whereas Ovid's tongue is firmly in his cheek. Similarly in lines 9–10, referred to in question 2 in the pupil's text, Penelope, the archetypal example of a faithful wife, is mischievously used by Ovid to exemplify a supremely difficult challenge for a would-be seducer. It is not hard to see why the *Ars Amatoria* was a contributory cause of Ovid's exile. While Augustus was embarking on a programme of moral reform, Ovid was burlesquing the highly respectable genre of didactic poetry, which usually dealt with such edifying themes as agriculture and astronomy, and transferring its characteristic mixture of maxims, mythological allusion and scientific observation to the world of seduction and intrigue.

Adventurous teachers might ask the class whether they agree with Ovid's implicit generalisation about women, that they can always be won if the wooer persists long enough.

The picture in the pupil's text (p. 41), from a fifteenth-century manuscript of Ovid, actually accompanies the *Metamorphoses*; do pupils feel it is equally (or more) suitable as an illustration for the *Ars*?

Suggestions for consolidation: ablative of comparison (two examples in line 7, cf. 'Catullus' I, p. 32, line 14); future participle (2).

Vocabulary check: *spērō* (2); *patior* (4); *magis* (7); *dūrus* (7, 8); *mollis* (7, 8).

Vergilius (*Aeneid* III.192–206)

Commentaries: Williams (large commentary on *Aeneid* III, shorter notes in his commentary on *Aeneid* I–VI), Page.

The following is one possible sequence of operations for reading this passage:
1 the teacher might add further comment to the introduction in the pupil's text, explaining that Troy has been destroyed by the Greeks, and the Trojans are in search of a new home;
2 teacher and class explore the glossary together;
3 the teacher reads the passage aloud;
4 pupils answer the 'A' questions orally or in writing;
5 pupils work out the translation together under the teacher's guidance, with the translation of some difficult phrases put on the blackboard for subsequent reference;
6 further exploration, using some of the 'B' questions;
7 a final reading aloud of the text, by teacher or possibly pupils.
When exploring the glossary, the teacher might point out that one reason for its length is the use of some familiar words with new meanings; examples might be discussed with the class. The connection between the two glosses on *volvere* could be explored, as could the link between the glosses on *caecus*, and their connection with the literal meaning (cf. 'blind corner').

Notes

1 **nec . . . ūllae:** translation initially difficult, but straightforward when sense has been established by comprehension questions.

5 **magna:** predicative ('the seas were running high', Day Lewis); cf. *servus mortuus prōcubuit*, *lupus superior stābat*, etc.

10 **negat:** cf. *rūmor tam bona vīna negat* ('Mārtiālis' I, p. 36, line 2). **caelō:** unfamiliar use of ablative; use context to establish meaning. (Local ablative will be discussed in a language note in Stage 47, when the pupils have met more examples of it.)

11 **Palinūrus:** postponed subject may cause difficulty, though the footnote in the pupil's text should help. If necessary, give further aid by asking 'What does Palinurus do in line 10?'

15 **vīsa:** (sc. *est*) governs *sē attollere* in 14, *aperīre* and *volvere* in 15. Again, the context can be used as a guide to the meaning. Virgil's description should touch a chord of recognition in any pupils who have approached a coast from the sea, and watched the land first appear as a smudge on the horizon, then reveal hills, cliffs and

other geographical features, and finally houses and people (cf. question A10).

Questions A4 and B2 can be used to explore Virgil's evocative description of the sea in lines 4 (*inhorruit*) and 5 (*ventī volvunt mare*); members of the class should be invited to draw on the blackboard their idea of the sea's appearance, as described in each of these lines. Encourage pupils to pick out the various elements in the scene suggested by *inhorruit*, such as the shivering surface of the ocean, the sound of a choppy sea and the white caps of the waves visible among the *tenebrae*. Do they feel Virgil also suggests a responsive shudder in the sailors?

Pupils might be asked 'What aspect of the storm does Virgil emphasise most strongly? the violence of the wind? rain? darkness? the roughness of the sea?' Ask them to pick out some of the words and phrases by which the darkness is emphasised.

For helpful suggestions for other possible questions, see Tingay, *Comprehendite* 83.

The class might be divided up into small groups for discussion of questions B3 and B5, as suggested on p. 23 above. Pupils often begin by assessing the literal accuracy of the rival translations; concern for accuracy is of course no bad thing, but encourage them to see that there are also other points at issue in translating poetry. If B5 is too vague, rephrase it in more specific terms on the lines of B3. The compactness of Latin emerges from a comparison of the number of words used in lines 12–13 by Virgil and his translators: for Virgil's 12 words, Dryden has 13, Jackson Knight 24 and Day Lewis 20. Has Dryden missed anything out? Have Jackson Knight and Day Lewis added anything? Is Virgil more succinct than his translators, and does this make his lines more effective, or less? Question B5 could also lead to discussion of the meaning of *incertōs* (line 12) and the way the translators have handled it. Does it mean (as Page says) that the Trojans couldn't tell when it was day and when night, or (as Williams says) that throughout they were in a state of total uncertainty and bewilderment, not just about the time?

The picture is from a fourth-century mosaic discovered at Low Ham, Somerset, and shows the Trojan ships landing at Carthage. On the right, Achates lands with a necklace as a gift for Dido; the reason for his curious position, apparently on his back, is that he also belongs in the adjacent mosaic picture, which is at right angles to this one.

Suggestions for consolidation: 1st person plural passive endings (6,9); expressions of time (12–13, 14); variation of nominative-accusative-verb word order (1, 5, 7).

Vocabulary check: *undique* (2); *aequor* (6); *auferō* (8); *cursus* (9); *negō* (10); *meminī* (11); *errō (13); sīdus* (13); *procul* (15).

Second language note (verse word order)

Encourage pupils to read each line of verse through at least twice, noting the more easily identifiable case-endings as they read, then to check the other case-endings if necessary before attempting a translation. The various examples provide useful incidental practice in recognising cases (especially nominative, accusative and ablative) of both nouns and adjectives.

It is desirable for the pupils to notice some of the effects created by the verbal patterning in these lines of verse, and not attribute the word order to clumsiness or perversity on the poet's part. For instance, the close collocation of two contrasted adjectives might be noted in the first example in paragraph 2, and pupils should be able to spot for themselves the similar effect in paragraph 4, example 2. They might note, too, that it is often the two adjectives that are placed early in the line, while the two nouns, which generally carry more of the emphasis, are held back to the end, as in paragraph 2, example 1, where the line is rounded off by the juxtaposition of the two beasts, killer and killed.

The English verse in paragraph 3 is from Gray *Elegy written in a Country Churchyard*. For comment on the similarity between the patterns created by rhyme in English verse and those created by noun and adjective phrases in Latin, see Unit IVA Handbook, pp. 39–40.

Manipulation exercises

Exercise 1 Type: vocabulary
Linguistic feature being practised: meanings of *ēmittere*, *petere* and *referre*

Some of the examples in this exercise have more than one possible answer. Similar practice can of course be given with other verbs, e.g. *agere* (see Language Information section of pupil's text, p. 220).

Exercise 2 Type: completion
Missing item: verb
Criterion of choice: morphology
Linguistic feature being practised: 1st, 2nd and 3rd persons singular and plural, future passive of 3rd and 4th conjugation verbs

Direct the pupils if necessary to p. 190 of the Language Information section.

Exercise 3 Type: transformation
Linguistic feature being practised: indirect statement with present passive and future active infinitives, introduced in Stage 38

The background material

The time-chart draws together and supplements various pieces of chronological information scattered through previous Units, and puts the five poets of Stage 42 in their historical context. (A similar chart, with a larger number of authors but without the list of historical events, appears in Stage 46.) It is sufficiently brief for dates and events to be copied by pupils into exercise books, if the teacher wishes, so that further items of information can be added to the chart from time to time.

Pupils might be asked what other historical events or names of Roman authors they can recall; their dates (exact or approximate) can then be related to the information in the time-chart. If the teacher wishes to list the names of first-century emperors on the blackboard, they are probably easier for pupils to assimilate if they are presented in three groups: Julio-Claudians; emperors of the A.D.69 civil war; Flavians.

Connections can be explored betwen the dates of the poets and the historical information presented in the chart. 'Of the five poets listed here', it might be asked, 'Which one lived entirely in the Republican period? Which poet lived under most emperors?' The problems faced by Martial and his contemporaries during the more autocratic phase of Domitian's rule could be considered, and the sycophancy of some of Martial's writing might be recalled from Unit IVA. If the question is asked, 'Who had more extensive experience of living through civil war, Virgil or Ovid?', discussion might develop into a comparison between Virgil's commitment to the Augustan régime and Ovid's more detached or subversive attitude, which led eventually to his punishment.

Vocabulary checklist

Discussion of *caecus* might refer to its occurrences in 'Vergilius', p. 42, lines 9 and 12. The pair of cognates *caecus–caecitās* can be compared with *vīlis–vīlitās*, which were met in the previous checklist; and for *reperiō–repertor* cf. *vincō-victor*, *scrībō–scrīptor*, etc., including harder examples such as *augeō–auctor*.

Suggestions for further work

Present the class with duplicated copies of an extract from George Orwell's *Animal Farm* or William Golding's *Lord of the Flies*, Coleridge's epigram, 'Swans sing before they die – 'twere no bad thing/Did certain persons die before they sing', a piece of versified weather-lore such as 'Red sky at night . . .' (or, as a closer parallel to Ovid, Sir John Suckling's 'Song', 'Why so pale and wan, fond lover?'), and extracts from Henry King *The Exequy* (or Auden *In Memory of W. B. Yeats*) and John Milton *Paradise Lost*. (Alternative examples can of course be easily substituted; for instance, there is a rich store of didactic verse in Brett's anthology.) Without telling the class which is which, indicate that each example belongs to the same type or family as one of the Latin poems in Stage 42, and ask pupils to match each English example with the corresponding piece of Latin.

STAGE 43: ŪNIVIRA

Synopsis

Reading passages	Petronius, *Satyrica* 111–12 (adapted) extracts from *I.L.S.* 8393 (*laudātiō Tūriae*) (adapted)
Background material	divorce and remarriage
Language notes	imperfect subjunctive passive genitive and ablative of gerund position of verb of speaking, asking, etc. with indirect statement and question

The reading passages in this Stage consist of two sharply contrasting treatments of the themes of love, marriage, fidelity and bereavement. The first, taken from Petronius' satirical novel, is fictitious, cynical and light-weight; the second passage, based on an inscription, is historical, tender, affectionate and serious.

Title picture

This affectionate husband and wife date from the Republican period and are now in the Museo Vaticano.

mātrōna Ephesia I (Petronius, *Satyrica* 111–12)

The teacher could supplement the introduction in the pupil's text with a brief comment on Petronius, e.g. by reading Tacitus' colourful obituary of him in *Annals* XVI.18–19 (attractively translated by Balme, *MDP* 8). It might also be explained that the *Satyrica* is a huge episodic narrative of the travels and escapades of a disreputable hero and his hangers-on, parodying romantic fiction and adventure stories and greatly influencing later writers from Cervantes in *Don Quixote* to James Joyce in *Ulysses* (for the episodic structure, cf. television soap opera); the present episode is a story-within-a-story, narrated by one of the hero's friends to the captain of the ship on which he and his companions are travelling.

There are some trickily long sentences in the passage (see Notes below), but other sections are sufficiently easy to be handled by phrase-by-phrase translation in the way described on p. 1 above.

Notes

3–5 **nōn modo ... prōsecūta est:** Remind class of the importance of reading the clause right through to the end before attempting a translation.

5 **sepulcrō:** It is of some relevance to the story that a tomb in Roman times could be large and relatively comfortable; cf. the illustration in pupil's text (p. 52).

11–12 **cīvibus affirmantibus:** ablative absolute pendant to the rest of the sentence. It might be translated literally at first, and pupils then be asked for idiomatic versions.

14 **prōvinciae:** Asia.

15–19 **proximā ... fieret:** It may be helpful if the teacher reads the whole of this long sentence aloud to the class, then asks comprehension questions on it, before (or instead of) having it translated. A good class may be able to understand much of the sense while listening to the teacher's reading with their books closed, if given some help with key vocabulary in advance (see pp. 2–3 above).

16–17 **nē corpora ... dētraherentur:** The humiliation of public exposure and non-burial (or delayed burial) of the corpse was an important element in crucifixion. As an example of non-burial of an offender, some pupils may know of the Antigone myth; see also the narrative in the Gospels (e.g. *Mark* 15.42–6) for Joseph of Arimathaea's special application to the Roman governor for the crucified body of Jesus.

29 **eīsdem blanditiīs:** Help will probably be needed with the form

and meaning of *eīsdem*, and with the relationship of *eīsdem blanditiīs* to *quibus* in line 30. Comprehension questions such as 'What did the soldier begin to do? How?' might be used.

Some suggested questions

Why was the lady praised by all the women of Ephesus?

How did she behave at her husband's funeral? (For the flamboyance and uninhibited nature of ancient mourning, cf. Stage 42, p. 32, lines 4–5 and p. 34, line 9. For a full account of the ritual, see Toynbee 43–55, Paoli 128–32 and C.S.C.P. *The Roman World, Handbook 2*, 123 and 126, and for a picture of a funeral procession, the Amiternum relief shown in (e.g.) C.S.C.P. *The Roman World* 5b, Paoli 124, Tingay and Badcock 84 and Balme, *MDP* 20–1 and described in detail by Toynbee, 46–7.

What orders did she give to her slaves?

Whose appeals did she reject? What had she decided to do?

How long did she go without food? What did the people say about her?

Why was the soldier near the tomb at night?

What attracted him to the tomb? What attracted him to the lady?

What arguments did he use to get the lady to eat? What did he mean by *inānī* (line 23)? What do you think of his arguments?

How did he persuade the lady to agree to his next request?

Suggestions for consolidation: locative (1; see also Language Information, p. 206); substantival participle (18, 22, 23; see also Language Information, p. 211 of pupil's text and p. 130 below). There are several opportunities to revise more basic points, such as time phrases (7, 11, etc.; accusative and ablative usages are contrasted in Language Information, pp. 204–5), participles (3, 4, etc.; for example, the class might be asked whether *cōnfecta* agrees with *inediā* in 26) and various uses of *ut* (2, 3, 4, 5). A 'question-per-line' approach can be adopted, e.g.:

What is the antecedent of *quae* in 1?
Why is *laudārētur* (2) subjunctive?
What case is *marītō mortuō* (3)? etc.

Vocabulary check: *quīdam* (1, 16); *propter* (1); *mōs* (4); *īdem* (5, 29); *ūnā* (6); *coepit* (7, 23, 30); *cōnstituō* (9); *vērus* (12); *praestō* (13); *interim* (14); *lūgeō* (15); *ēligō* (16); *gemitus* (18); *cognōscō* (19); *fīō* (19); *cōnsistō* (20); *iaceō* (33). Special attention might be paid to the disentangling of *cōnsistō* and *cōnstituō*.

mātrōna Ephesia II (*Satyrica* 112)

Notes

6–7 **mātrōnae . . . exposuit:** Use the captioned line drawing in the pupil's text to help with the word order. The postponement of a verb of speaking or asking, so that it follows an indirect statement or question, is discussed in a language note later in the Stage.

8–9 **potius sē . . . esse:** indirect speech continued from previous sentence. Cf. *omnibus . . . pereundum esse* in 'mātrōna Ephesia' I, p. 54, line 24.

14–15 **illī quae . . . crucī:** Use question 6 in the pupil's text, expanded if necessary, to help the class with the postponed antecedent.

Question 8 usually leads to lively discussion. The teacher might quote the comment of the sea captain to whom the story is related, that if the commander of the soldiers had been an honourable man he would have put the dead man back in the tomb and nailed the woman to the cross. The class could also be asked 'What else could the woman have done? Should she have allowed her new lover to go ahead and kill himself?'

Question 9 may provoke a variety of answers: the neat way in which the corpse of the woman's first love becomes the means of saving the life of her second; the complete reversal of the woman's attitude during the course of the story; the interwoven themes of love and death, with the former ultimately triumphant. Adverse comment is, of course, 'permissible'; pupils should be free to say, if they wish, that the story has been overrated. Some classes will enjoy pursuing the question 'Is this story a sexist joke?' Relevant here are the irony of *nōn minus misericors quam pudīca* (lines 10–11) and the identity of the story's narrator (the homosexual Eumolpus) in its original context in the *Satyrica*. (If a positive answer has been given to question 8, it could be argued that Eumolpus' sexist gibe misfires.)

Details of other versions of the story are given in Sedgwick (141). The diction of Christopher Fry's play on the subject, *A Phoenix Too Frequent*, would make it hard going for most pupils unless they have a fairly sophisticated experience of modern verse plays; but they might enjoy reading the closing pages, from the re-entry of the soldier Tegeus after he has discovered the theft of the body from the cross. (Fry's play, unlike the present adaptation, follows Petronius in including a third character: the kindly maidservant who encourages her mistress.)

Suggestions for consolidation: perfect passive participle in accusative (3; see also Appendix B); ablative of time (1, 11).

Vocabulary check: *ūnā* (1); *auferō* (4); *supplicium* (6); *vereor* (6); *accidō* (7); *negō* (7); *īdem* (11); *mālō* (12); *ūtor* + ablative (16).

First language note (*imperfect subjunctive passive*)

If (as is usually the case) these endings have caused no trouble when met in 'mātrōna Ephesia', it could be pointed out to the class that they have already seen several examples of the imperfect subjunctive passive and translated them successfully, probably without even realising that they were meeting anything new.

Many of the suggestions made in connection with the present subjunctive passive (p. 24 above) are equally applicable here. Pupils might be referred to Part III of their Language Information section and use the infinitive forms there listed of (e.g.) *laudō*, *redūcō* and *tangō* to deduce the subjunctive forms for 'they were being praised', 'we are being led back', 'I was being touched', etc.

After studying p. 198 of the Language Information section, some pupils will be able to make appropriate comment on the deponent verbs with little or no prompting: e.g. that as usual the forms are passive but the meanings active, and that if the endings *-r*, *-ris*, etc. are removed, a present active infinitive form invariably appears.

Tūria I (*I.L.S.* 8393, I.3–8, IIa.2–5, II.5–7)

The passages in the pupil's text are based on the inscription traditionally known as the *laudātiō Tūriae* (*I.L.S.* 8393, *C.I.L.* VI.1527, 31670 and 37053). The bulk of this inscription is on two stone slabs which were originally tightly juxtaposed and may have formed an integral part of the tomb of the woman commemorated by the inscription; possibly it was carved in situ, with the stonecutter crouching or lying on the ground to complete his work. Other smaller fragments of the inscription have also been discovered, one of which is shown in the photograph on p. 67 of the pupil's text (see pp. 53–4 below for a transcription and translation).

The inscription itself is the record of a spoken *ōrātiō*, delivered by the husband of the dead woman. The version in the pupil's text is a free adaptation, loosely based on *I.L.S.* 8393 but making large omissions and including some material from other sources. It was long believed that the speaker of the *ōrātiō* was the Quintus Lucretius, whose adventures, together with those of his wife Turia, are the subject of lively accounts in Appian, *Civil Wars* IV.44 and Valerius Maximus VI. 7.2 and who was further identified with the Lucretius Vespillo who was consul in 19 B.C. These identifications, however, have now been generally rejected, most recently by Horsfall, who points out that the speech in *I.L.S.* 8393 shows an absence of political involvement and family pride, as well as evidence of some deficiencies in the speaker's rhetorical education, so that the speaker is most unlikely to be an ex-consul. The use of 'Vespillo' and 'Turia' in the pupil's text is purely for the convenience of having names to refer to.

Lewis and Reinhold I.484–7 and Lefkowitz and Fant 208–11 contain translations of the bulk of the inscription. There is an engaging (if somewhat rose-tinted) account of it in Warde Fowler 159–67, and there are helpful discussions in Balsdon *RW* 204–5 and Lefkowitz's *Greece and Rome* article (31–47, especially 42–4). Horsfall's article, to which these notes are much indebted, is not easily accessible but contains the fullest and most recent discussion.

The text, even in its adapted form, contains some difficult patches, and the teacher should be ready to intervene if the pupils are getting bogged down (see p. 3 above).

Notes

1–2 **utrōque parente ... occīsīs:** perhaps by their slaves.

3 **mors ... mānsit:** It is worth reminding pupils that Turia at this time might still have been in her teens or early twenties. She is debarred from speaking in court because of her sex, but is still able to play a leading role in the proceedings – a nice illustration of the point that a woman's power and position in classical times did not depend wholly on her legal status.

4–5 **efflāgitandō ... investīgandō ... ulcīscendō:** the first appearance in the pupil's text of the ablative form of the gerund. The first example is glossed, and pupils should have no difficulty in working out the other two examples by analogy.

5–6 **sī adfuissem ... potuissem:** conditional sentence with pluperfect subjunctive; the apodosis is translated in the pupil's glossary. There is no need to discuss it further with pupils at this stage; it will be the subject of a language note in Stage 46.

13–14 **inter cameram ... cēlātum:** This detail comes not from the inscription but from Valerius Maximus VI.7.2; it illustrates the shifts to which the proscribed and their families were put. Pupils may enjoy spotting Vespillo in the picture on p. 59 of their text.

14–15 **tanta ... cōnārēris:** The 2nd person singular form of the imperfect subjunctive of a deponent verb is likely to cause pupils some hesitation; the picture may provide a helpful reminder of the context.

Some suggested questions

What disaster happened to Turia on the eve of her wedding? (If the pupils need more help, ask a series of simpler questions, e.g. 'What did Turia suddenly become? When? How? Where did it happen?' etc., and similarly with the questions that follow.)

Why was Vespillo unable to help her in avenging her parents?

What two qualities did Turia display? What compliment does Vespillo pay to her efforts?

When Vespillo fled for his life, what practical help did Turia provide (a) at the time (b) regularly thereafter?

When Vespillo was declared a 'public enemy', how did his friends react? What was Turia's advice? Where did she hide Vespillo? Why does Vespillo say that she was acting *nōn sine magnō perīculō* (line 15)?

The most suitable topic for exploration in this passage will probably be the historical background. Some of the following material might be read to (or studied by) the class:

the proscription edict (Appian, *Civil Wars* IV.8–11, quoted by Lewis and Reinhold I.301–3);
the adventures of some of the proscribed (e.g. from Appian *Civil Wars* IV.37–51);
the humiliating treatment of 'Turia' by the triumvir Lepidus, and her eventual success in seeking an amnesty for her proscribed husband (from a section of *I.L.S.* 8393 not included in the pupil's text, given in Lewis and Reinhold I.486, Lefkowitz and Fant 210).

Suggestions for consolidation: predicative dative (7); dative pronoun and participle at head of clause (7, 9); perfect passive participle in accusative (8, 14; see also Appendix B); 1st and 2nd persons singular, perfect passive and deponent (1, 12); purpose clause with relative pronoun (8).

Vocabulary check: *fīō* (1); *uterque* (1); *maneō* (3); *officium* (3); *adsum* (5); *amplius* (5); *auxiliō est* (7); *praebeō* (10); *vītō* (11); *patior* (12); *cēlō* (14).

Tūria II (*I.L.S.* 8393, II.25–7, 31–6, 40–7)

Most pupils will again need help from time to time with this passage.

Notes

3 **precibus . . . fortūna fāvisset:** word order may catch the unwary.

3–4 **fāvisset . . . cupīvissēmus:** conditional sentence with pluperfect subjunctive (see note on p. 46 above, on 'Tūria' I, lines 5–6).

4 **annīs . . . lābentibus:** If pupils are baffled, it may be best to elicit a literal translation first and then encourage a more idiomatic one.

6–8 **diffīdēns . . . īnfēlīx:** After the teacher has read this aloud, comprehension questions could be used: 'What was Turia pessimistic about? What saddened her? What fears did she have about Vespillo?' etc.

10–11 **tē ipsam . . . esse:** indirect statement continued from previous sentence. Ask the class 'Who will find the worthy wife? Is this Vespillo's own statement or is he reporting Turia's words? How can you tell? How will Turia regard the children of the new marriage?'

12 **quibus verbīs audītīs:** cf. *quibus verbīs dictīs*, 'mātrōna Ephesia' II, p. 55, line 13.
incēnsus sum: cf. *servātus sum*, 'Tūria' I, p. 59, line 12. The question 'What were Vespillo's feelings?' will bring out the point that Vespillo not only rejected Turia's suggestion, but was appalled by it.

The main point for discussion is likely to be Turia's proposal and Vespillo's reaction to it. What do the class feel about the contrasting attitudes of Turia and Vespillo? What might the reaction of their Roman contemporaries have been (this question could be used as either an introduction or a follow-up to the background material)? Might the men, paradoxically, have tended to agree with Turia, and the women with Vespillo? In particular, would men have disagreed with Vespillo's undervaluing of *necessitās habendī līberōs* in lines 13–14? (If so, why does Vespillo say in line 15 that divorce would have been a *dēdecus* to him?)

Some other points of detail might be explored:

What does *vacuam* (line 9) mean? (Questions like this are often worth asking, however obvious the answer may seem to the teacher. The pupils are likely to see the point if they are asked to consider it; but if their attention is not drawn to it, it probably won't occur to them.)

What does Turia mean by *dignam* (line 10)? What other qualities besides fertility might she look for in her successor?

What are Vespillo's four arguments against his wife's proposal? What does he mean by *fidem fallere* and *certa dubiīs* in line 14? Why does he break off in lines 14–15 with *quid plūra?* Does he feel that further details are irrelevant, or undignified?

Which word in lines 15–16 contrasts with *meō*, and which with *dolōre*? (The antitheses support the view that, in spite of the occasional clumsiness, this *laudātiō* is not a wholly artless piece of writing.)

Suggestions for consolidation: possessive dative (13).

Vocabulary check: *fruor* + ablative (2); *magis ac magis* (2); *līberī* (2); *teneō* (7); *fīō* (8); *audeō* (8); *dignus* (10); *quaerō* (10); *adeō* (12); *vix* (12); *maneō* (15); *cēdō* (15).

Tūria III (*I.L.S.* 8393, I.28–30, II.54, 58–60, 69)

Notes

1 **contigit nōbīs:** If this causes difficulty, pupils could be reminded of its occurrence in 'Tūria' II, p. 60, line 1. The *dī mānēs* may be recalled from their appearance on tombstones in Stage 28.

Some suggested questions

How long did the marriage last? What aspect of the marriage does Vespillo pick out for special comment? (Some alert pupils may spot the contradiction between Vespillo's phrase *sine ūllā discordiā* (1) and his previous account of the furious row with Turia over her suggestion of a divorce.)

Why had Vespillo not expected his wife to die before him? (It might be noted that the commonest reason in Roman times for a wife to predecease an older husband, death in childbirth, does not apply in this instance.)

What encourages Vespillo to struggle against his grief? What is his consolation? What is his final prayer?

Pupils might be invited to comment on the qualities for which Vespillo praises Turia; are some of them a little unexpected? Are they the same qualities as might be mentioned in modern times in praising a wife? (Some of the original Latin words might be studied: *pudīcitia, obsequium, cōmitās, facilitās, assiduitās lānificiīs, religiō sine superstitiōne, ōrnātus nōn cōnspiciendus, cultus modicus.*)

The drawing on p. 61 shows 'a virtuous woman spinning', based on a mosaic from North Africa. The woman is holding the distaff with her left hand and pulling out and twisting the thread with her right.

Suggestions for consolidation: possessive dative (6; see also 'Tūria' II, p. 60, line 13, and for further examples Language Information section, paragraph 5e on p. 205 of pupil's text, and p. 128 below).

Vocabulary check: *dolor* (3, 5); *aliquandō* (4); *ēripiō* (5); *adhūc* (6); *patior* (7).

Second language note (genitive and ablative of gerund)

Pupils will be reassured to learn that they have now met all forms of the gerund in common use, since it has no nominative and no plural, and the dative is rare.

Further examples:

1 *servus meus numquam artēs legendī et scrībendī didicit.*
2 *Vespillō, diū latendō, inimīcōs fefellit.*
3 *tantus erat strepitus ut amīcus noster nūllam occāsiōnem dormiendī habēret.*
4 *cōnsul, bellum callidissimē gerendō, hostēs tandem reppulit.*
5 *tacēte, puerī! nihil querendō efficitis.*
6 *omnēs mīlitēs studiō pugnandī ardēbant.*

Manipulation exercises

Exercise 1 Type: vocabulary
Linguistic feature being practised: synonyms

Pupils tend to muddle *fīdus* with *fidēs*.

Exercise 2 Type: completion
Missing item: verb
Criterion of choice: sense and morphology
Linguistic feature being practised: future tense
Incidental practice: conditional clauses, introduced in Stage 42

Exercise 3 Type: translation from English, using restricted pool of Latin words
Linguistic features being practised (relevant page of Language Information section given in brackets): 1st person plural imperfect passive (190); fear clauses (208, paragraph 7); ablative absolute (211, example 6); 4th declension (178); ablative of time (205, paragraph 6d); present infinitive (195), perfect indicative (197) and present indicative (196) of deponent verbs; *id quod* (187, paragraph 9).

Third language note (position of verb of speaking, asking, etc. with indirect statement and question)

The main point to stress is the need to read the sentence right through before translating. The rule 'first find the verb' is usually less helpful than an instruction to *notice* the verb of speaking, asking, etc. while reading through the sentence.

The tense of the verbs of speaking, etc. in paragraph 3 varies between present and past. The teacher may need to be on the lookout for any signs of insecurity in either recognising or coping with these tenses, and provide further examples if needed. Additional practice in handling *et ... et* may also be shown by sentence 6 to be necessary.

Pupils might note that it sometimes adds to the point and effectiveness of a sentence if the Latin word order is retained in translation:

quārē Imperātor Agricolam revocāverit, numquam sciēmus.
Why the emperor recalled Agricola, we shall never know.

rēgem rēctē occīsum esse, nēmō negābit.
That the king was justifiably killed, no one will deny.

For further examples, the teacher might refer pupils back to *mīles, quī mātrōnam esse ... animadverterat* ('mātrōna Ephesia' I, p. 54, line 28) and *mātrōnae quid accidisset exposuit* ('mātrōna Ephesia' II, p. 55, lines 6–7, with illustration).

The background material

On divorce and remarriage generally, Balsdon *RW* 209–23 is invaluable. There is a full account of the legal aspects in Corbett 218–51 and a crisp summary in Hammond and Scullard, s.v. *Marriage, Law of*, paragraph 8. Crook 105–6 is useful, and Carcopino 109–15 is lively and readable, if somewhat rhetorical and over-ready to trust Martial and Juvenal as evidence. Williams quotes Aulus Gellius' account of the Carvilius divorce in full (*Tradition and Originality* 372), and discusses Virgil's use of Roman marriage concepts, including the *ūnivira* ideal and the de facto nature of Roman marriage, in *Tradition and Originality* 374–87 (73–7 in abridged version).

The Juvenal quotation in the pupil's text is from *Satires* VI.225ff. 'They marry to divorce, divorce to marry' is Seneca, *De Beneficiis* III.16.2. The Zois and Antipater divorce agreement is given in full in Lewis and Reinhold II.407–8; it is apparent from the complete text that the marriage had lasted less than a year.

The most interesting way to approach the topic is probably to look at particular instances of divorce in Roman times, especially involving individuals mentioned elsewhere in the Course or otherwise known to the pupils. In some cases, pupils could find out the details themselves, with the aid of references supplied by the teacher, and report their findings back to the class. For example:

The tempestuous marriage of Quintus Cicero and Pomponia, an incident from which was described in Unit IVA, p. 76, ended in divorce in 45 B.C. Quintus contemplated remarriage, but decided against it, remarking that life offered no happiness greater than a single bed (Cicero, *Ad Atticum* XIV.13.5).

The marriage of Quintus Cicero's more famous brother Marcus to Terentia lasted for thirty years but eventually broke up. Of the twenty-four surviving letters he wrote to her, the earlier ones (especially those written from exile) are affectionate, but the tone grows distinctly cooler as the marriage deteriorates; in the end, believing she was swindling him, he divorced her. Being then in acute difficulties over the repayment of her dowry, he married the young and wealthy Publilia, only for this marriage, too, to collapse in a few months, leaving Cicero's financial problems unabated.

When P. Clodius, a young man of colourful reputation, was discovered disguised as a girl in the house of Julius Caesar during a religious rite from which men were excluded, it was claimed he was having an affair with Caesar's wife Pompeia. Caesar thereupon divorced her, but declared he did not believe the accusation himself, and on being asked 'In that case, why the divorce?' made his famous remark that Caesar's wife must be above suspicion. (Mention of Clodius in this incident may help pave the way for the appearance of his sister in the background material of Stage 45.)

The five marriages of Pompey (two terminated by death, two by divorce and the last by his own death) illustrate not only the exploitation of marriage and divorce by Roman *nōbilēs* for political reasons but also the fact (exemplified in Pompey's marriage to Caesar's daughter Julia) that a marriage arranged out of political calculation can still be characterised by strong mutual affection.

If the inscription *C.I.L.*V.5279 refers to the father of Pliny the Younger (a disputed attribution), the marriage of Pliny's parents ended in divorce, and his father went off to live with a concubine called Lutulla, by whom he had two sons.

Lewis and Reinhold I.508–9 quote from Valerius Maximus' collection of instances in Republican times where a husband divorced his wife for trivial or eccentric reasons, such as visiting the games without his knowledge or going out with her head uncovered. Perhaps few of these anecdotes are authentic; but they illustrate the Romans' belief that in Rome's earlier days male dominance had emphatically been the norm in marriage.

Generally, the law was more insistent on formalities and public proceedings for ending a marriage *cum manū* than a marriage *sine manū*. (Augustus made a short-lived attempt to extend the formalities to *sine manū* marriage, for example by requiring a declaration of divorce before witnesses.) If the wife had been married *cum manū*, her husband, if he wished to divorce her, had to take the necessary legal steps to transfer her to the *manus* of somebody else, either a member of her own family or an appointed guardian. Whether the marriage was *cum manū* or *sine manū*, the return of part or all of the dowry to the woman's family was crucial, to help her to secure a second marriage. Pupils may note that the dowry of Zois, in the divorce document quoted in their text (p. 67), was relatively paltry; if she had been a member of a powerful dynasty of Roman *nōbilēs*, the dowry would have been much more substantial.

Seneca, *De Matrimonio* 72–7, quoted by Balsdon *RW* 208, records several anecdotes illustrating Roman regard for *ūnivirae*. But the social and economic pressures for marriage (and remarriage) meant that there was a sizeable gap between preaching and practice. Rudd, 42–7 (in an interesting discussion of Dido's actions in *Aeneid* IV) suggests that by the time of Augustus, *ūnivirātus* enjoyed a sentimental esteem as a pleasant if rather old-fashioned ideal, but that this respect for *ūnivirātus* had little significant effect on people's behaviour, nor was there much disposition to blame a widow if she remarried. Augustus himself had no doubts about the matter. His marriage legislation imposed financial penalties on childless widows between the ages of 20 and 50 if they failed to remarry within a year from their husband's death, and he made frequent use of divorce and remarriage in his own family when the political occasion required; for instance, his daughter Julia was married first to Marcellus, then on Marcellus' death to Agrippa, then on Agrippa's death to Tiberius, who had himself been forced to divorce his existing wife.

The photograph on p. 67 of the pupil's text shows one of the smaller fragments of the *laudātiō Tūriae*. Scholars have made various suggestions for the missing portions but the text remains disputed and the interpretation unclear. The transcription and translation below are an attempt at a coherent version, based on the edition of Durry. The first five lines provide the basis for lines 7–10 on p. 59 and pupils might enjoy picking out various words and phrases with the teacher's help.

V]XORIS

AMPLISSIMA SUBSI]DIA FVGAE MEAE PRAESTITISTI ORNAMENTIS;
VT EA FERREM ME] CVM, OMNE AVRVM MARGARITAQUE CORPORI
TVO DETRACTA TRADI]DISTI MIHI ET SUBINDE FAMILIA NVMMIS
FRVCTIBVS,
CALLIDE DECEPTIS A]DVERSARIORVM CVSTODIBVS, APSENTIAM
MEAM LOCVPLETASTI.
VITAM TVTATA APSEN]TIS, QVOD VT CONARERE VIRTVS TVA TE
HORTABATVR,
PIETAS TVA TE M]VNIBAT CLEMENTIA EORVM CONTRA QVOS EA
PARABAS:
SEMPER TAMEN V]OX TVA EST FIRMITATE ANIMI EMISSA.
INTEREA AGMEN EX REPER]TIS HOMINIBVS A MILONE QVOIVS
DOMVS EMPTIONE
POTITUS ERAM CVM ESSET] EXVL BELLI CIVILIS OCCASIONIBVS
INRVPTVRVM
ET DIRECTVRVM PROSPERE REIECISTI ATQVE DEFE]NDISTI DOMVM
NOSTRAM.

To the memory of my wife

With the aid of your jewellery you provided the utmost help for my flight; you took off all the gold and pearls from your body and handed them to me so that I could take them with me, and on numerous occasions, cleverly deceiving our enemies' guards, you enriched me in my absence with household slaves, money and provisions.

While guarding my life when I was away – it was your courage that urged you to these efforts – your loyal devotion protected you through the mercy it inspired in those against whom you were laying your plans. But always you spoke out with steadfastness of mind.

Meanwhile, when a troop of men collected by Milo (whose house I had acquired by purchase when he was in exile) were about to break in and plunder, taking advantage of the opportunities of civil war, you successfully beat them back and defended our home.

Suggestions for discussion

1 Why did the Romans like to think that divorce was not introduced into Rome until the 3rd century B.C., whereas in fact it had already existed for two centuries by that date? (This could lead to discussion of the Romans' tendency to idealise their early past as a moral Golden Age; do other societies similarly idealise the past?)

2 Why is there no masculine equivalent for *ūnivira*?

Vocabulary checklist

The teacher might check pupils' understanding of the difference between *magistrātus* and English 'magistrate'. With *ulcīscī–ultiō–ultor* cf. *scrībere–scrīptiō–scrīptor, dēfendere–dēfēnsiō–dēfēnsor, coniūrāre–coniūrātiō–coniūrātor*, etc.

Suggestions for further work

For examples of funerary inscriptions which could be studied, discussed and compared with 'Tūria' (especially Section III), see Lewis and Reinhold I.489, II.283–6, and the inscriptions in C.S.C.P. *The Roman World*, e.g. nos. 1, 2, 5, 7, 9, 11, 14, 16.

STAGE 44: DAEDALUS ET ĪCARUS

Synopsis

Reading passages	Ovid, *Metamorphoses* VIII.183–235
Background material	Icarus in art
Language notes	historic present omission of word from one of two clauses 3rd person plural perfect in *-ēre*

Ovid's tale of Daedalus and Icarus has a clear narrative structure, blends humour with pathos and can appeal powerfully to the imagination. It also presents the pupils with a more substantial verse extract than those of Stages 36, 39 and 42, and paves the way for the increased complexities of the verse in Stages 45 and 47. The illustrations and background material use the Icarus episode to exemplify the potency of classical myth as a source of inspiration to later artists and writers.

Part I (*Metamorphoses* VIII.183–9, 191–2)

(The obscure and probably corrupt line 190 has been omitted.)

Hollis' commentary will be very helpful throughout this Stage.

The title of Ovid's poem ('changes of shape') could be explained to the class; it might be added that Ovid uses ingenious digressions and transitions to include several stories which do *not* contain a metamorphosis (such as the present episode of Daedalus and Icarus, unless one regards it as a tale of metamorphosis from man to bird). The class could also be told some of the earlier parts of the story, such as Pasiphae's infatuation with the bull, the birth of the Minotaur (and perhaps his killing by Theseus) and Daedalus' construction of the labyrinth. The king's refusal to allow Daedalus to leave was a punishment for facilitating Pasiphae's union with the bull. The map in the pupil's text (p. 73) should be used to establish some basic data: that Crete is an island, that Daedalus' home town was Athens, etc.

Notes

1–2 **longum . . . exilium:** In dealing with these and other split phrases, the class will be helped by careful phrasing when the teacher reads the text aloud, and by periodic reminders that each phrase or sentence must be read through to the end. See also 'Suggestions for consolidation' below.

3–4 **clausus erat pelagō . . . undās obstruat:** Not only is Crete an island, but also Minos has many ships at his command.

6 **dīxit et . . .:** Encourage the class to discard literal renderings in favour of 'So he spoke, and . . .' or 'When he had said this, he . . .', etc.

8–9 **clīvō . . . avēnīs:** The range of uses of the ablative is a feature of Latin verse with which pupils need to become familiar; this familiarisation is inevitably fairly slow and gradual. It is better at this stage *not* to draw up lists of different ablative usages, as this merely disheartens the pupils by opening up an apparently infinite field of possibilities. Instead, encourage them to use the context as a guide to the required meaning, and discuss the variety of usage when they have encountered many more examples; some comment appears in a language note in Stage 47.

Initially, it will be advisable to maintain a brisk pace and concentrate on establishing the narrative, postponing detailed exploration of the text until pupils have become more used to Ovid and his language. Focus on Daedalus' wish to escape, his reasons for choosing to escape by air, and the making of the wings.

Comprehension questions can highlight the precision of Ovid's account in lines 7–9: 'What was the first thing Daedalus did with the feathers? In what order did he arrange them? What appearance would they have had to an onlooker?' Guide the class to visualise the arrangement of feathers in order to interpret the difficult phrase *ut clīvō crēvisse putēs* ('the feathers seem to have grown naturally (*crēvisse*) in order of ascending length (*clīvō*)' (Hollis)). If they are puzzled, use the simile that follows for clarification; ask 'What exactly is the point of similarity between the wings and the Pan-pipes?' and invite volunteers to draw both wings and pipes on the blackboard.

Suggestions for consolidation: Throughout this Stage, there are opportunities to practise split phrases, in which an adjective is separated from the noun it describes and noun + adjective phrases are juxtaposed or intertwined with each other, as described in language notes in Stages 36, 39 and 42 (see above on lines 1–2). When the passage has been read and discussed, examples of split phrases (e.g. those in lines 1–2, 6, 8–9, and 9, some of which are underlined to help the pupil) can be picked out for the class to study, read aloud or retranslate, identifying the case and sometimes noting the effect achieved by the phrase (e.g. the highlighting of the key word *ignōtās* in line 6).

Vocabulary check: *intereā* (1); *pelagus* (3); *unda* (3); *animus* (6); *pōnō* (7).

Part II (*Metamorphoses* VIII.193–202)

Notes

1	**adligat:** to be taken twice over; both ablatives qualify both accusatives.
4	**ignārus:** used in a way unfamiliar to pupils, to introduce indirect statement. Use question 2 to establish the sense, or ask the class to identify the case of *sē* and form of *tractāre*.
5–8	**ōre ... opus:** Several comprehension questions will be necessary before any attempt at translation is made. The first part of question 3 can be developed and expanded: 'What were the two things Icarus did? Which feathers was he trying to catch? What was he doing to the wax?' etc.
9	**lībrāvit:** Pupils are usually slow to see that this governs *corpus*. Ask 'What did he balance?' and if they say 'The wings', tell them to take a second look at line 10.

The blackboard diagram mentioned above in connection with Part I could now be elaborated, with a pupil marking in the wax and thread at appropriate points. The class might be asked, on *parvō curvāmine* in line 2, 'What was bent, the wings' edge or their surface?'

Ovid's description of Icarus playing is noteworthy not only for its homely and sympathetic realism, but also because the characterisation of Icarus paves the way for the eventual tragedy, and lends it plausibility; there is pathos, too, for those who are aware (as presumably all Ovid's original listeners were aware) that Icarus is doomed. Question 2 might be expanded by a further question, 'Does Icarus understand at all what is going on?', to bring out the significance of line 4 ('If he only knew what he was fooling with, he would stop fooling at once!'). The fact that Icarus is too young to be expected to behave responsibly – and is therefore all the more of a risk on the journey – could be elicited by asking 'Does Ovid suggest that Icarus is doing all this out of naughtiness?' or 'Why does Daedalus not rebuke his son?' The pupils may be able to pick out such phrases as *ōre renīdentī* (line 5) and *lūsū...suō* (line 7), which make it clear that to Icarus his father's activity is simply a new and agreeable game.

Question 4 seeks to establish that Daedalus, having constructed the wings, is carefully executing a trial run. If the class are asked to describe his action in detail, this will help them to feel the vividness and tension of Ovid's narrative. The moment when Daedalus puts his whole weight on the wings (*lībrāvit in ālās*, line 9), the steady beating of the air (*mōtā*, line 10), and the hovering (*pependit*), are all described crisply and effectively.

The picture in the pupil's text shows Michael Ayrton's bronze, 'Daedalus winged'. The teacher might simply ask the class to describe the bronze, helping them if need be with such questions as 'What moment in the story do you think the bronze illustrates?' 'Suggest a reason for the posture in which Daedalus is standing.' 'Do Ayrton's wings differ from the description in the Latin?'

Suggestions for consolidation: perfect passive participle in accusative (2; see also Appendix B); split phrases (3, 4, 5, etc.; see 'Suggestions for consolidation' on Part I, p. 56 above).

Vocabulary check: *cēra* (1, 6); *compōnō* (2); *vērus* (3); *opus* (8); *āla* (9); *pendeō* (10).

Part III (*Metamorphoses* VIII. 203–9)

Notes

1 **et:** postponed. Compare the use of *-que*.

1–2 **'mediō ... moneō':** The interweaving of direct speech and narrative, and the displacement of *ut*, may cause difficulty. The teacher might read the sentence right through to *moneō* and then ask 'What did Daedalus say?'

2 **moneō:** placed after the indirect command which it governs. Perhaps try a simpler example, with the subject expressed, e.g. *centuriō mīlitibus ut pugnārent imperāvit*, or *senex puerōs ut festīnārent monuit*.

5 **iubeō:** See previous note.
strictumque Ōrīonis ēnsem: It will probably have to be explained to the class (preferably by an astronomically-minded pupil, if the class contains one) that Orion with his sword is a prominent constellation in the south, useful to navigators.
6 **mē duce:** Parallel examples (*Eleazārō duce*, *mē auctōre*, etc.) could be recalled from previous Units.

Some suggested questions

What advice did Daedalus give to Icarus?
What were the dangers of going too low or too high?
How would Icarus know which way to go?
What else was Daedalus doing while giving this advice?
Which word in line 7 highlights the idea of danger?
Why is Daedalus' advice so detailed, and why does he repeat himself (*mediō* ... *līmite* in line 1; *inter utrumque* in line 4)? Is he just a fussy old man? Is he shrewdly aware of the importance of repetition when giving instructions? Is he desperately trying to explain a highly risky situation to someone too young to understand it? Is the point being emphasised because Ovid wants to prepare the reader (or listener) for the story's eventual climax?

For a note on the Greek vase fragment on p. 76, see the background material in the pupil's text, p. 87, and p. 65 below.

Suggestions for consolidation: gerund (6); split phrases (1, 5, 7).

Vocabulary check: *penna* (3); *uterque* (4); *nec* (4); *aut* (5); *āla* (7).

First language note (historic present)

The class could pick out further examples of the historic present from the opening lines of Part II (p. 74) and the end of Part III (p. 76), noting that it can be used alongside perfect or imperfect tenses (as in the example in paragraph 1, and the lines referred to in paragraph 4). It might be pointed out that the historic present occurs in English as well as Latin, though less frequently. Often it is colloquial ('I was standing on the corner when all of a sudden this car draws up and three men jump out', etc.).

Part IV (*Metamorphoses* VIII.210–20)

Notes

4 **comitīque timet:** first occurrence of *timeō* used with the dative. Attention to the context, and to the case of *comitī*, should make the meaning clear.

5 **quae:** appears unusually late in its clause. Careful phrasing by the teacher will help.

7 **ālās:** object of both *movet* and *respicit*. The teacher might first put *movet ipse suās ālās* on the board for translation, then add *et nātī respicit ālās*, and finally remove the first *ālās* as superfluous. Sentences like these are discussed in the next language note.

8–11 **hōs . . . deōs:** a complex sentence. After the glossary has been studied, and the lines read aloud by the teacher, one way of proceeding is to put questions to the class about the scene described by Ovid. Such questions can both help to establish the surface meaning and add to the pupils' appreciation of the poetry. For example:

Teacher: Who are the three people mentioned here? . . . What are they doing? . . . What does Ovid say about the fisherman? . . . *Why* was the rod quivering? . . . (*Pupils:* He's catching a heavy fish . . . he's surprised at the sight of the aeronauts.) . . . What about the other two people? What are they doing? . . . Does *innīxus* refer to the shepherd, the ploughman, or both? . . . Why are they leaning on the staff and plough-handle? . . . (*Pupils:* . . . to get a better view of Daedalus and Icarus . . . they've just stopped to take a breather.) Does the next line help you to decide? . . . (*Pupils: vīdit* comes after the description of the two men, so the shepherd must have been leaning on his staff already, when Daedalus and Icarus came into view.) Does that help to explain the fishing-rod? . . . (*Pupils:* . . . he was catching a fish; that's why the line was quivering – and then as he hauled the fish out his gaze moved up from the water and he saw the aeronauts.)

Such an approach is in fact exploring the precision and vividness of Ovid's description without ever using such terms explicitly. It is probably a better approach than 'How skilfully does Ovid describe the scene?' and certainly better than 'Notice how good Ovid is at visual description.'

10–11 **quīque . . . deōs:** relative clause placed before main clause and antecedent. Question A4 may be of help.

In looking for points of similarity between the aeronauts and the birds, in answer to question B2, the pupils might be led from the more obvious points ('Both pairs are flying'; 'Both pairs are parent-and-child') to the physical resemblances in the situation ('The elder leads the way, looking back continually at the weaker member – *teneram* – and demonstrating the art of flight') and the similarity of emotion (*comitīque timet*, line 4, applicable both to Daedalus and to the mother-bird). Abler pupils may be able to spot not only the similarities but also a significant difference: the situation of the bird and nestling is a natural one, whereas that of Daedalus and Icarus is not.

ōscula ... nōn iterum repetenda (lines 2–3) and *damnōsās* (line 6) will readily be found by the pupils when they search for overtones of disaster in answer to question B3; they might also be guided to the ominous implications of *crēdidit esse deōs* in line 11 (in the world of classical mythology, it is ill-advised for mortals to usurp the attributes of gods).

The teacher might need to draw pupils' attention to the fact that the wall-painting reproduced on p. 79 is a composite picture, showing two different stages of the story. Icarus is depicted twice, once in the top right-hand corner falling out of the sky and again as a corpse in the centre at the bottom. This is clearer in slide IV.1. Do pupils think it would have been better to have painted *two* pictures, on adjacent panels of the wall, or is something gained by showing both stages within a single picture? Encourage the class to describe the painting in their own words, perhaps noting how the painter has built up a context for Icarus' death: not just sky and sea but a walled town on an island, men in boats (perhaps they have just retrieved the corpse?) and a sacred pillar in the foreground by the spectators.

Suggestions for consolidation: 4th declension nouns (1, 2); split phrases (1, 2, 2–3, 4–5, 6, 8).

Vocabulary check: *opus* (1); *gena* (1); *penna* (3); *comes* (4); *hortor* (6); *āla* (7); *aliquis* (8); *aethēr* (10).

Part V (*Metamorphoses* VIII.220–35)

Question A1 in the pupil's text might be discussed as soon as lines 1–3 have been read. Ovid locates the scene of the catastrophe fairly precisely, partly to conform to the requirements of the myth and partly to spell out the circumstances of the tragedy ('So much had been safely accomplished, and so much had still to be done, when disaster struck.'). Some pupils may ask why Daedalus and Icarus, after flying steadily towards Athens, have swerved unexpectedly eastwards. The closing lines of the section will reveal an explanation. The class could be asked why Ovid adds *Iūnōnia* (line 1) and *fēcunda . . . melle* (line 3) (on the use of adjectives to add variety to a string of names, see p. 31 above).

Simple comprehension and linguistic questions may be helpful in dealing with lines 4–9. For example:

Which verb tells you Icarus' feelings in line 4? Which adjective describes his flight?

What did he do to his leader? Does 'left him behind' mean that he overtook him, or something more?

Tingay *Comprehendite* 79 is a useful source of ideas for further questions.

Lines 10–11 are the hardest lines in this section, partly because of the intertwining of nouns and adjectives, and partly because Ovid is combining two points; the description of Icarus, shouting till his cries are stifled in the water, merges into the explanation for the name of the Icarian sea. Question A4 could be expanded by asking 'Was Icarus already dead when he hit the water? How do you know?' followed by 'Where did Icarus fall? What was the name of the sea?' Further study of the map should now clear up the puzzle about the aeronauts' route which was left unresolved at lines 1–3, and the role of myth in explanations of place-names could be explored.

One or two of the following questions could also be considered:

'Why does Ovid describe Daedalus in line 5 as *ducem* rather than *patrem* (which he in fact wrote in his earlier version of this story, *Ars Amatoria* II.84)?' Possible answers might include the alliteration with *dēseruit* (used, as often by Ovid, to mark a key moment in a story), and the use of *ducem* to indicate the role that rightly belonged to Daedalus (cf. *mē duce*, Part III, p. 76, line 6).

'What is the point of *odōrātās* in line 7?' ('Proleptic – the smell of the wax is brought out as it melts in the sun': Hollis.) If the teacher asks 'Has Ovid suggested earlier that the wax was easily softened?' pupils may be able to point back to *mollībat* in Part II, p. 74, line 7. Discussion of the tense of *tābuerant* (line 8) may help to bring out the rapidity with which Ovid's narrative moves at this point.

'In what sense were Icarus' arms bare (*nūdōs*, line 8)? Does *quatit* refer to his attempts to stay airborne or is he trying to attract attention?'

'How can the same word (*rēmigiō*, line 9) mean both wings and oars? What is the point of similarity?' On metaphor generally, see p. 4 above. Hollis compares the movement of a bank of oars beating the water to the movement of wings beating the air. There may also be irony in Ovid's choice of 'oars' as a metaphor for wings; oars (and a boat) are very much what Icarus now needs.

'How appropriate or otherwise is the repetition of *dīxit* (lines 12–13) and the change to *dīcēbat* (line 14)?'

'Is Icarus' behaviour here consistent with what we have been told about him previously?' Pupils generally decide that Icarus' irresponsible adventurousness here fits well with his playfulness in Part II; but they also often feel that there has been a shift in Ovid's presentation of him, from child to young man.

Before question B3 is tackled, all five Parts might be rapidly re-read, with the teacher perhaps doing most of the translation but requiring regular contributions from the class. The question 'Should either of the characters be blamed for the accident?' might be answered by referring to the indications of Icarus' impetuosity in Part V, p. 80, lines 4–5 or to Daedalus' self-recrimination, p. 81, line 15, and the hints in Part IV, p. 78, lines 1–2, that he foresaw the tragedy. Ovid himself, though showing plenty of sympathy for Daedalus' and Icarus' feelings, nevertheless adopts the conventional attitude of the ancient world to 'tampering with nature' (cf. *ignōtās* in Part I, p. 72, line 6 and Part III, p. 76, line 7, *nātūram . . . novat* in Part I, p. 72, line 7, etc.).

The class could be asked whether they sympathise with one character more than the other. Some may see Icarus as a rash fool; others may find Daedalus' cautious attitude irritating, no less so when justified by the event. Some may see the characters as 'types' – the Cautious Father and Impetuous Son. The teacher might ask, 'Why does the young man reject the fruits of his father's greater experience? Is this far-fetched or is it like real life? Would it be better if youth *always* listened to the cautious advice of older generations?', etc.

The question 'Describe what you see in this picture' is particularly useful with the painting reproduced on p. 80 and could also be used with other illustrations in this Stage. Pupils are very familiar with looking at pictures, on television and elsewhere, and are often quicker than adults at spotting visual details. On Allegrini's painting, they might be asked 'Does the picture help to explain why Icarus came to grief but Daedalus escaped?' 'Are the two spectators on the promontory behaving differently from the others?' 'In what ways does this painting differ from the Pompeian wall-painting (p. 79)? For example, which painting gives more sense of spaciousness?'

Vocabulary check: *coepī* (4); *ūllus* (9); *excipiō* (11); *īnfēlīx* (12); *unda* (14).

Second language note (omission of word from one of two clauses)

Simpler examples of this point were given in the Language Information pamphlet of Unit IIB (p. 22) and the Teacher's Handbook for Unit IVA (p. 15), and could be used (or re-used) here if necessary. Stress the importance of reading the sentence through to the very end before attempting translation. If the class find paragraph 5 difficult, examples 3–8 can be expanded by the teacher in the same way as examples 1 and 2. The expanded version could be put up on the blackboard in stages; for instance, in example 3 the teacher could write up *nōs in urbe habitāmus*, then add *vōs prope mare habitātis* and finally remove *habitāmus* (cf. note above, p. 59, on Part IV, line 7). When the pupils have grasped the point, they can be asked to work out the expanded version for themselves, inserting the word that has to be 'supplied' from one clause to another. Encourage them to compare the relative effectiveness of the 'shorter' and 'longer' versions of each example; they are usually quick to see that the 'shorter' version, though harder to translate, sounds neater and more forceful.

Further examples:

1 *culpam mīlitēs in servōs, servī in mīlitēs trānsferre poterunt.* (Stage 41, p. 6, lines 7–8)
2 *Fortūna multīs dat nimis, satis nūllī.* (Martial)
3 *dum caelum stēllās, dum vehit amnis aquās.* (Tibullus)

Manipulation exercises

Exercise 1 Type: vocabulary
Linguistic feature being practised: meanings of *solvere*

Exercise 2 Type: completion
Missing item: adjective
Criterion of choice: sense and morphology
Linguistic feature being practised: agreement of noun and adjective

Competent and ambitious pupils could be allowed to complete some or all of the sentences with adjectives of their own choice, not taken from the pool. *longus* (in pool) is sometimes muddled with *longior* (Language Information section, p. 182).

Exercise 3 Type: transformation
Linguistic features being practised: 1st and 2nd persons singular and plural, present, future and imperfect passive, introduced in Stages 35 and 39; ablative singular and plural

The exercises in the Language Information section, p. 190, paragraph 2, may be helpful as either an introduction or a follow-up to this exercise. Pupils tend to have difficulty with the meaning of *moritūrus*, and consequently the tense of *sepelient*, in sentence 3a.

Exercise 4 Type: completion
Missing item: infinitive phrase
Criterion of choice: sense and morphology
Linguistic feature being practised: indirect statement

For further practice, see Language Information section, pp. 209–10, paragraphs 1 and 3.

Third language note (3rd person plural perfect in -ēre)

The most convenient way of practising this ending is to concentrate on the point which is most likely to worry pupils – the possibility of confusion between this form and the infinitive. The teacher could select a number of verbs from Part III of the Language Information section, asking the class to pick out the infinitive of each verb and then to give the verb's 3rd person plural perfect form in *-ēre* (easily deducible from the 1st person perfect form, listed immediately after the infinitive); the two forms, and their respective translations, may then be compared. This exercise can also give useful incidental practice of verbs whose perfect stem causes problems of recognition; for example, the class might study such pairs as *agnōscere* and *agnōvēre*, *scindere* and *scidēre*. Finally the teacher could give a mixture of assorted infinitive and 3rd person plural *-ēre* forms (e.g. *exercēre*, *iussēre*, *servāvēre*, etc.) for the class to recognise and translate, using the Language Information section if necessary.

For a brief account of the use made of the *-ēre* perfect form by Roman writers, see R. D. Williams (large commentary) on Virgil, *Aeneid* V.580.

The background material

Martindale, *Ovid Renewed* 247–53 has a very helpful survey of treatments of the Daedalus and Icarus myth in art.

The date of the vase-painting in the pupil's text (p. 76) might be stressed, to make the point that the myth was not invented by Ovid but was already of great antiquity when Ovid wrote.

Ayrton's work was dominated for ten years by the Daedalus myth, his interest being aroused not by Ovid but by Virgil's account in *Aeneid* VI.14ff. Another of his treatments of the Icarus theme is shown in slide IV.3.

When considering Bruegel's painting, the class might be encouraged to comment on the behaviour of the bystanders (who ignore Icarus' fall completely, unlike the spectators in the other paintings) and the extreme lack of emphasis on Icarus himself (it may take pupils some moments to find him). Why do the class think Bruegel called his painting 'The Fall of Icarus' and then paid so little attention to him? Judging from the picture, do the triumphs and tragedies of manned flight matter less than the everyday business of real life? Is the German proverb 'No plough stops just because a man dies' relevant? Is this also the point of Auden's poem? Or are Auden and Bruegel suggesting that people just want to get on with their own lives, rather than become involved in other people's tragedies? In which picture is Icarus' fate sadder – the Pompeian wall-painting, where he is surrounded by people who grieve for his death, or the Bruegel painting, where nobody wants to know? Perhaps (as Morford suggests) the painting, with its emphasis not on Icarus but on the labouring ploughman, owes less to Ovid than to Virgil's *Georgic* I, with its theme of the importance of hard toil: '*labor omnia vincit improbus*' (145–6).

Suggestions for discussion

1 Of the various treatments of Icarus in art, which did you most like or dislike, and why? (It may be worth emphasising to the class that there was never any 'standard' version of the myth; each artist, including Ovid and Auden, handled the myth in the way that most appealed to him, choosing details that he wanted to use, rejecting others and inventing further ideas of his own.)

2 Suggest reasons why this story has appealed to so many artists and been retold so often. (Rudd in Martindale 21–53, has a rich store of examples. Pupils should, between them, be able to suggest several reasons; that the story is visually dramatic, for example, or that the characters are easy to relate to or sympathise with, or that the story involves strong emotions. The teacher might mention that, for similar reasons, many other stories in the *Metamorphoses* have exerted a strong influence on later art and literature; examples of such stories could be quoted by the teacher, and where the story is known to any members of the class they could retell it to the rest in outline form.)

Vocabulary checklist

The pair of cognates *vincīre–vinculum* can be compared with *vehere–vehiculum*, *spectāre–spectāculum*, *mīrārī–mīrāculum*, etc.

Suggestions for further work

Ovid's text could be considered from the point of view of a director making a film of the episode. Which moments might be treated by long-range shots, and which by close-ups? How can the similes in Parts I and IV be effectively realised on screen? How should the geographical details in the final section be visually indicated? The class could draw up their own scripts, describing their choice of successive shots with notes and/or sketches, and adding ideas of their own for such matters as musical accompaniment, 'zooming' shots, fade-outs and fade-ins, and special visual effects. They often show considerable expertise over technical points, and sometimes take great pains to produce work which is meticulous, sophisticated and (in spite of occasional gimmickry) effective.

STAGE 45: LESBIA

Synopsis

Reading passages	Catullus, *Poems* 51, 5, 3, 70, 72, 85, 8, 11
Background material	Clodia (Cicero, *Pro Caelio* 30–2, 49, 59–60 in translation)
Language notes	jussive subjunctive relative clauses with antecedent deferred or omitted dative of disadvantage

---

The theme of the eight poems in this Stage is Catullus' love affair with Lesbia. The subject-matter generally appeals to adolescent readers, and much of the verse is linguistically straightforward. Roman numerals indicate the numbers assigned to these poems within Stage 45; Arabic numerals indicate the standard numbering system used in (e.g.) the Oxford Classical Text edition.

The poems can be read as a sequence: first encounter of Catullus and Lesbia – mutual love – Catullus' suspicions – his conflicting feelings – the end of the affair. Such a sequence makes things easier for the pupils on their initial reading, but begs a number of controversial questions. During or after their reading of these poems, the pupils might consider what we know (or do not know) about the order in which the poems were written, and their relationship (if any) with events in Catullus' life.

Title picture

Based on a first-century painting of a girl decanting perfumes, from the Villa Farnesina on the right bank of the Tiber, and now in the Museo delle Terme, Rome.

I 'ille mī pār esse ...' (*Poem* 51)

The commentaries of Fordyce and Quinn will be helpful throughout this Stage; so will Wiseman 130–82. References to other books and articles are given below from time to time in connection with individual poems. On the present poem, see Lyne *Handbook* 25ff. and G. Williams *Tradition and Originality* 251f. (55f. in abridged version); Williams also discusses several other poems in this Stage.

Notes

1 **ille:** Encourage the class to leave this initially as an unexplained 'he'; then, when line 3 is reached, indicate that *quī ... audit* supplies the explanation.

2 **superāre:** When pupils have realised the line is incomplete as it stands, a reminder of line 1 will probably enable them to see that *vidētur* is the word to be supplied.

5 **quod:** postponed. Comprehension questions, such as 'What does this do to Catullus?', may help.

5–6 **miserō ... mihi:** Encourage pupils to discard initial literal translations, e.g. 'miserable me', in favour of more idiomatic versions, e.g. 'me in my misery'.

7 **aspexī:** 'Have set eyes on' may prepare the pupils better than 'set eyes on' for the present tenses which follow.

9 **sed:** postponed to second word. Note how the class are coping with this feature, which they have now met several times, and give help if necessary.

9–10 **tenuis ... flamma:** separated. Encourage the class to read right through to *dēmānat* before translating.

15 **et ... et:** Pupils tend to go astray through assuming that the first *et* links *ōtium* with *rēgēs*. A simpler example may help, e.g. *dominus et servōs et ancillās laudāvit.*

Discussion might begin by asking 'Who do you think *ille* is? Is he a real person? Which word in the first stanza indicates that *ille*, whether real or imaginary, enjoys a permanent relationship with Lesbia?' Two points of interpretation could also be considered: 'Is *sī fās est* (line 2) short for *sī fās est dīcere* or for *sī fās est dīvōs superāre*?'; 'To what does *quod* (line 5) refer?

The attractive laughter? The sight of Lesbia? The sight of Lesbia in the presence of another man?'

The second part of question 1 could be amplified by asking 'Why can Catullus not enjoy what the other man enjoys?', which might lead to a discussion of the other man's status (husband, established lover, etc.). Discussion of question 2 (e.g. argument over whether *tenuis flamma* and *sonitus* are examples of 'loss of sense') will help to clarify Catullus' picture in lines 7–12. The teacher might add the further question: 'Is Catullus' description convincing? If it's not physically true, does it nevertheless give us a clear idea of his feelings?' Rudd and Foster, in a helpful discussion in Greig 42–8, suggest the question 'Do these lines describe painful or pleasurable feelings?'

For opposed views on the status of the fourth stanza, referred to in question 3, see Fordyce *ad loc.* and Lyne *Handbook* 27–9. Encourage the airing of both points of view: that this is a coherent poem, in which Catullus feels he is being carried away by emotion, and writes a final stanza of warning to himself on the traditional theme of *ōtium* as a cause of *amor*, decadence and disaster (see, e.g., Balme and Warman 106–7 for documentation of this theme); or that the contradictions between the address to Lesbia and the self-address to Catullus, and between the passion of lines 1–12 and the moralising of 13–16, indicate that we have here not one poem but two, attached to each other in the manuscripts because of their identical metre.

This may be a suitable point in discussion for the teacher to reveal that the poem is substantially a translation of a Greek poem by Sappho of Lesbos. (The class might consider whether the case for accepting lines 13–16 as part of the poem is weakened by the fact that they correspond to nothing in the original Sappho.) Wilkinson, quoted by Quinn *Catullus* 241, suggests that the poem leaves Lesbia free to take it either as an exercise in translation or as a declaration by Catullus. Catullus' decision to translate a Sappho lyric can be considered in conjunction with his choice of 'Lesbia' as a pseudonym for the woman he is addressing; choice of Greek original and choice of pseudonym can be taken to imply that the woman is appreciative of lyric poetry and that she is beautiful, like the women of Lesbos whom Sappho wrote about. It could also be mentioned that 'Lesbia' has been identified with a woman called Clodia; the names 'Lesbia' and 'Clodia' are metrically interchangeable, and so Catullus would have been able to substitute the real name for the pseudonym when he read his poems aloud to her.

Vocabulary check: *pār* (1); *identidem* (3); *ēripiō* (6); *aspiciō* (7); *ōs* (8); *ōtium* (13ff.); *molestus* (13); *et . . . et* (15).

II 'vīvāmus, mea Lesbia . . .' (*Poem* 5)

Bramble's discussion in Greig 18–22 usefully complements Quinn and Fordyce.

Notes

1–3 **vīvāmus . . . assis:** Perhaps best handled by a series of comprehension questions. 'Who is Catullus addressing? What does he say they should do? What else?', etc. Question 1 in the text should enable pupils to cope with the separation of *rūmōrēs* from *omnēs* in lines 2–3.

5 **nōbīs:** The most convenient translation may be the literal one, 'for us'.

6 **ūna:** perhaps surprisingly, often causes trouble. Ask the class 'How many nights?'

10 **fēcerīmus:** Pupils will need to be guided to idiomatic translations, 'we have had', 'we have exchanged', etc.

11–13 **nē sciāmus . . . bāsiōrum:** On first reading, it is probably better not to get over-involved in explanation of these lines. Establish the main point, 'lest we, or anyone else, should know the number', then explore the lines in more detail later; see below.

A second reading might combine translation with exploration. Get the class to work out the translation of lines 1–6, and then to tackle question 2. Translation of lines 7–9 could be followed by question 3, with the teacher giving help if the pupils are slow to see that human mortality is being used by Catullus as an argument to Lesbia: 'Life is short, let us enjoy it while we can.' Similarly, translation of lines 10–13 might be followed by exploration of question 4, to which the class could find a variety of answers: that it is not very lover-like to ration one's love; that an infinity of kisses is better than a finite number; that to know and state the precise amount of one's good luck is dangerous, since it invites Fortuna to sweep it away. The shift at the end of the poem could then be discussed. Not only are Catullus and Lesbia not to know the number, but neither is anybody else, partly because Catullus and Lesbia would be objects of envy (*invidēre*, line 12) and partly because of the primitive belief that to have exact knowledge of personal details about other people gives power over them, enabling an ill-wisher to cast the evil eye on them (another meaning of *invidēre*).

One or two of the following questions could also be considered:
'Since there is only one sun, why is *sōlēs* (line 4) plural?'
'What does *lūx* (line 5) refer to?'

'Which words in lines 5–6 contrast sharply with each other? What do you notice about the way Catullus has positioned *lūx* and *nox*?' (Or the point could be explored the other way round by asking 'How does Catullus emphasise the contrast between *lūx* and *nox*?')

'Study Catullus' use of numbers in this poem; how do they help him to emphasise what he is saying to Lesbia?' The class might notice the juxtaposition of *ūnius* with *omnēs* in line 3, and the contrast between *ūna* in line 6 and the vast and ever-increasing numbers in lines 7–10, also the regular pattern in those lines, contrasting with the idea of disruption in line 11?

'How did the ancient world keep count? Why would it be easy for Catullus to upset the reckoning (line 11) with a single movement?' For details of the abacus, see *Omnibus* 5, p. 4.

'Does the *malus* in line 12 remind you of anyone Catullus has mentioned earlier in the poem?' The repetition of the idea of a critical or jealous observer, in lines 2 and 12, strengthens the unity of the poem, as does the recurring 'numbers' motif.

'How does the situation described in this poem differ from that of the previous one ('ille mī pār esse . . .')?' For evidence that Catullus is now no longer a tongue-tied outsider, as in the previous poem, pupils might be able to point both to the confident tone of his invitation and to the suggestion in lines 2–3 that his relationship with Lesbia may now be a subject of public gossip.

Balme and Warman 40–2 have an interesting trio of translations of lines 1–6, for comparison. A musical setting of the poem, composed by a pupil for voice and guitar accompaniment, appears in *Omnibus* 10, p. 16.

The marble pair shown in the photograph on p. 94 and from the Capitoline Museum is thought to be a Roman copy of a late Hellenistic work of the 2nd or 1st century B.C. It is usually interpreted as Cupid and Psyche. In some versions of the pair the figures have wings.

Vocabulary check: *vīvō* (1); *brevis* (5); *scio* (11, 13); *malus* (12).

First language note (jussive subjunctive)

Further examples:

1 *castra hostium oppugnēmus; aut occīdāmus aut occīdāmur.*
2 *amēmus patriam, pāreāmus senātuī.* (Cicero)
3 *nē haesitet amīcus vester.*
4 *vīllam ingrediāmur; nē diūtius in hortō morēmur.*

With help from the teacher, the class might work together to produce a translation of Cato's instructions about the bailiff:

5 *haec erunt vīlicī officia: aliēnō manum abstineat; sua servet dīligenter; vīlicus nē sit ambulātor* ('be always wandering off'); *sobrius sit semper.*

The jussive subjunctive provides a convenient opportunity for pupils to practise the difference between present indicative and present subjunctive forms in each conjugation by translating paired examples such as *recitāmus–recitēmus*, *trahāmus–trahimus*, etc. The conjugation to which each verb belongs could be either indicated by the teacher or found out by pupils for themselves by consulting Part III of the Language Information section.

Invite comment on the tone of the two examples in paragraph 3; for example, do the class feel that the jussive is gentler or ruder than the imperative as a way of ordering people around?

III 'lūgēte ō Venerēs ...' (*Poem* 3)

Lyne *Handbook* 6–9 and Balme in Greig 6–12 have useful comments on the poem.

Most of the following questions could be answered by pupils without further help after initial study of the glossary and reading aloud of the whole poem by the teacher:

Who are addressed in line 1? What are they asked to do?

Who else are to mourn? Why?

How is it described?

How fond of the bird was Lesbia? (Pupils may need help with *illa* in line 5, unemphatic 'she'). Why? How well did it know her?

How can we tell from line 8 that it was very tame?

What actions of the sparrow are described in lines 9–10? (If the class have trouble with *modo ... modo*, remind them of the boy Icarus in Stage 44 (p. 74, lines 5–6), *modo* chasing feathers, *modo* playing with wax.)

Translate *it* in line 11. Explain in your own words where the sparrow is going, then translate Catullus' description of its journey (line 11) and destination (line 12). (Pupils may need further help. They often say 'deny a return to anyone'; draw the case of *quemquam* and form of *redīre* to their attention.)

Whom does Catullus curse in lines 13–14? What does he say about them? What in particular have they done?

Whom does he address at the end of line 16? What does he call it?

What has been the effect of the sparrow's death on Lesbia? (Remind the class to read lines 17–18 right through to the end, to help them cope with the delayed subject of *rubent*.)

The class might then read the poem through again on their own, before proceeding to translation, a second reading-aloud or further exploration. Question 2 may provoke more than one answer: the Venuses and Cupids, as deities of love, may be invoked because Lesbia loved the sparrow and/or because Catullus loves Lesbia. The attempts of ornithologists to identify the bird from the clues in lines 8–10 might be mentioned. It is unlikely to be a sparrow, since sparrows are virtually impossible to tame. Fordyce 87–8 has a full discussion of the rival candidates, favouring the Italian blue rock-thrush, *monticola solitarius*, of which there is a good picture in Bruun and Singer 255. But 'sparrow' has, over the centuries, become the traditional translation for the most famous pet bird in European literature. (For a similar 'wrong' tradition, cf. the spelling 'Virgil' for Vergilius.)

A fruitful topic for discussion, to which question 5 might lead, is Catullus' attitude to the bird's death. Is the poem a genuine lament? Does Catullus share Lesbia's grief? Is he trying to cheer her up? Is it a love poem disguised as a lament? Pupils are often good at picking out the affectionate phrases of pathos in lines 6, 9–10, etc., and contrasting them with the mock solemnity of the addressees in lines 1 and 2, the mock-heroic or bathetic line 11 (in which the onomatopoeic *quī nunc it per iter* reinforces the somewhat absurd picture of the sparrow hopping down the dark road to Hades), and the (mock?) indignation against Hades and the sparrow in lines 13 and 15–16, all of which might suggest that Catullus' laments are not to be taken too seriously. The change of mood between lines 10 and 11, referred to in question 5, is taken by some pupils as a move from pathos to farce, by others as a move from lightness to seriousness (cf. lines 12 and 14); the point is worth debating. Questions 3 and 5 sometimes evoke from pupils the suggestion that Catullus is obliquely reproving Lesbia for being too absorbed in the bird's death and inattentive to Catullus; for this view, cf. Lyne *Handbook*, especially 8–9. (Do pupils take *miselle* in line 16 as sympathetic or abusive?)

The assonance of the repeated 'l's and 'm's in this poem might be discussed (cf. the comments on 'Catullus' II in Stage 42, p. 33 above). So might the phrase *plūs . . . oculīs suīs* in line 5: is this just a poetic cliché, or does Catullus say anything later in the poem to give the phrase special appropriateness? Pupils are also often intrigued and amused by the old theory that *passer* is an obscene double entendre for *mentula*.

For a reproduction of a mediaeval manuscript of Catullus, showing the first five lines of this poem, see *Omnibus* 9, p. 19, and for interesting sets of comprehension and exploratory questions see Tingay *Comprehendite* 67 and Balme and Warman 19.

The winged cupids in the fresco from Herculaneum shown on p. 96 are playing what was apparently a popular children's game, in which two boys holding either end of a long rope tried to catch and tie up others who hit out at the pursuers with sticks.

Suggestions for consolidation: *negō* (12; both translations might be practised); ablative of the gerund (18); diminutives (16, 18); ablative of comparison (5; see also Language Information, p. 205 of pupil's text and p. 128 below). *male sit* (13) could be translated literally and linked with the note on the jussive subjunctive.

Vocabulary check: *lūgeō* (1); *plūs* (5); *modo . . . modo* (9); *iter* (11); *illūc* (12); *unde* (12); *malus* (13); *fleō* (18).

IV 'nūllī sē dīcit . . .' (*Poem* 70)

Notes

1 **nūllī . . . mālle:** The placing of the dative at the front of the sentence and the embedding of *dīcit mulier mea* inside the indirect statement usually cause problems. Comprehension questions may help: 'Who is speaking? Who is she speaking about? What does she say about herself?', etc.

3 **mulier . . . amantī:** Even with the help provided in the glossary, the word order is still likely to be difficult. Ask 'Who is the woman in line 3 talking to?', and for the use of *quod* compare a more familiar example such as *(id) quod dīcis falsum est.*

4 **scrībere oportet:** In the absence of an accusative, the Latin is ambiguous. It can mean both 'she (i.e. the woman) should write' and 'one (anyone) should write'. Perhaps a passive rendering ('ought to be written') best preserves the ambiguity; it is in any case the translation most likely to occur to the class.

The class might consider the real or imaginary situation envisaged in lines 1–2. Is the remark of *mulier mea* Lesbia's response to a serious proposal of marriage from Catullus? Is it a protestation of innocence in the face of Catullus' suspicions that she has other lovers beside himself? *nūbere* can be used of casual and temporary relationships as well as marriage (none of Jupiter's consorts, for example, was 'married' to him except Juno); which meaning(s) does the word have in the present context? Pupils could also discuss the appropriateness of the mention of Jupiter in line 2. His supreme status and desirability as king of the gods are obviously relevant; so, too, are his erotic adventures. Is the statement weakened by being put in the form of a (possibly trite) proverb, or is it appropriate to the hyperbole of lovers' talk? Is there a modern equivalent?

In answering question 2, pupils are sometimes attracted by the translation 'That's what *she* says' for the first *dīcit* in line 3; but this anticipates a scepticism which appears only later in the line.

Question 4 might be expanded in discussion. Does the image of wind and water mean that women's words are unreliable, unworthy to be permanently recorded in writing like the words of a marriage contract? What is the point of the reference to *cupidus amāns* in line 3? Does Catullus mean that it would be unreasonable to hold a woman to a statement which she's been badgered into making by her importunate lover?

If this poem belongs to a phase of the relationship where Catullus is becoming jealous and suspicious, could 'ille mī pār esse ...' (p. 92) belong to the same phase?

For further comments and suggested questions, see Lyne *Handbook* 13–15 and Balme *Intellegenda* 71.

The seduction scene shown on p. 98 has some extraneous features of interest which could be pointed out to pupils: the man reclining on his left arm in the customary manner, his drinking horn (rhyton), the very elegant table. Pupils may enjoy speculating about what is on the table or in the box that the servant girl is bringing.

Vocabulary check: *nūbō* (1); *mālō* (1; its derivation from *magis volō* could be mentioned, and various forms of *volō*, *nōlō* and *mālō* practised); *petō* (2); *oportet* (4).

V 'dīcēbās quondam ...' (*Poem* 72)

Notes

1–2 **dīcēbās ... Iovem:** Pupils should be able to recognise the statement attributed to Lesbia here as closely similar to the one quoted in the previous poem.

4 **ut:** postponed. *ut vulgus* in the previous line should help.

5 **impēnsius:** Pupils may need a simpler example of the comparative adverb, perhaps with *quam*, e.g. *Marcus celerius quam Sextus cucurrit.*

7 **quod:** not difficult to understand, but encourage the class to expand their translations to 'It is because ...' or similar.
amantem: substantival. Cf. *amantī* in line 3 of previous poem.

Question 2 could lead to discussion both of the simile's meaning and of its effectiveness. A father's love for his sons (with the spelling *gnātōs* adding an archaic flavour and increasing the emphasis by alliteration with *generōs*) is contrasted with the erotic feelings of a man for his mistress; the contrast is heightened by the addition of *generōs*. Has Catullus succeeded in conveying the idea of a love that is warm, intense and loyal, but to which sexuality is irrelevant? Or are Quinn and Lyne

(*Handbook* 15–19, *Latin Love Poets* 39–41) right to consider the simile a brave failure? Do the pupils find the description of Catullus' feelings in 3–4 convincing? Is it inconsistent with lines 5–12 of 'ille mī pār esse . . .' (p. 92)?

The middle section of question 3 might lead to consideration of the metaphor of *ūror*: 'What does Catullus mean by "being on fire"? What aspect of love is emphasised by *ūror*?', etc.

The structure of the poem is exceptionally clear. It abounds in pairs of contrasted words and phrases, and the class should be encouraged to pick some of them out. *quondam* (line 1) is first reinforced by *tum* (line 3) then contrasted with *nunc* (line 5). *ut vulgus amīcam* (line 3) corresponds with *pater ut gnātōs*, etc. (line 4). *impēnsius ūror* (line 5) expresses Catullus' increased passion, *multō . . . es vīlior et levior* (line 6) his increased distaste and contempt. In the final couplet, which describes the double result of Lesbia's infidelity and thus explains lines 5–6, *magis* contrasts with *minus*, and *amāre* with *bene velle*.

Vocabulary check: *quondam* (1); *dīligō* (3); *tantum* (3); *cognōscō* (5); *vīlis* (6); *tālis* (7); *cōgō* (8); *minus* (8).

Second language note (relative clauses with antecedent deferred or omitted)

It is often useful to the class to go through the further examples in paragraphs 1 and 2 picking out the antecedents, and also to practise translating *id quod* both literally ('that which') and idiomatically ('what'). Encourage idiomatic translations of *(is) quī* and *(eī) quī* ('the man who', 'people who', etc.).

For further examples of *is quī*, and relative clauses in which the antecedent is deferred or omitted, see Language Information, paragraph 9 on p. 187 of pupil's text and pp. 127–8 below.

Note how the class cope with the jussive subjunctive in paragraph 3, example 4, and make up further examples if necessary.

VI 'ōdī et amō . . .' (*Poem* 85)

Notes

1 **quārē:** The pupils have already met this word with its present meaning ('why'); but, having just encountered it in the previous poem with a different meaning, they may need help.

2 **requīris:** main verb placed after indirect question. Cf. language note on p. 65 of pupil's text.
fierī: impersonal passive. Encourage 'happen' or similar translation.

A famous and much-praised couplet. After it has been read and translated, pupils might be invited to demonstrate how they think it should be read aloud. The poem contains fourteen words: how many are strongly emotional, and where are they placed?

The poem makes no mention of Lesbia, but is usually assumed to be 'about' her; is this assumption reasonable? Is she the person addressed in line 1 (*requīris*)? Or is the addressee just an imaginary interlocutor, who enlivens the couplet by giving it the characteristics of a dialogue and providing a cue for Catullus to explain (or rather refuse to explain) his initial remark?

As in the previous poem, the class might note the extent to which Catullus' effect depends on antitheses: what examples can they find of pairs of contrasted or corresponding words? *ōdī* and *amō*, *nescio* and *sentiō*, should be picked out easily enough. An interesting contrast is that of *faciam* and *fierī*; to Catullus, hating and loving are not things that he does but things that happen to him.

The suggested alternative answers to the question in the pupil's text are not intended to exhaust the possibilities.

VII 'miser Catulle . . .' (*Poem* 8)

For detailed discussion, see Lyne (*Handbook* 20–5, *Latin Love Poets* 47–51) and G. Williams (*Tradition and Originality* 460ff.; 91ff. in abridged version).

Notes

1–2 Note how the pupils cope with the jussive subjunctives *dēsinās* and *dūcās*, and the omitted antecedent in line 2, and refer back to the language notes on pp. 95 and 101 if necessary.

3 **candidī:** predicative. Cf. *servus mortuus prōcubuit*, etc., and for further examples if needed, see Appendix B.

5 **amāta:** The use of the participle to add a further point often causes difficulty here. It may be helpful to ask 'Which word in line 4 is described by *amāta*? What does Catullus say in line 5 about the girl?'

9 **illa:** 'she'; cf. line 5 of 'lūgēte ō Venerēs', p. 96.
impotēns nōlī: Guide the class to see that *nōlī* picks up *nōn volt*

from earlier in the line, and that *impotēns* explains why Catullus is giving himself this advice.

10 **quae fugit:** For the positioning of the relative clause, and omission of the antecedent, cf. line 2.

17 **cuius esse dīcēris:** The teacher might compare a simpler example, e.g. *Lesbia mea esse dīcitur*, 'Lesbia is said to be mine'.

Exploration and discussion could be carried out along the following lines, with variation by teachers to suit their particular taste, pupils and circumstances:

After lines 1–8 have been translated, work through questions 1–2. ('Don't cry over spilt milk' is perhaps the most obvious answer to the second part of question 1, but others may occur to the class.) Then ask: do these lines refer to past, present or future? Why does Catullus call himself *miser*? Which of the first eight lines gives the strongest impression of Catullus' feelings about Lesbia? How is she described in that line? Which of them was the keener on the relationship? (There is room for argument here; line 4 suggests the harmony of their desires, but in line 7 he is eager while she merely acquiesces – unless the double negative *nec . . . nōlēbat* is interpreted as a strong affirmative.) What is the point of substantially repeating line 3 at line 8? (One answer might be that the reminiscence in lines 4–7 expands and justifies the claim in line 3, making its reiteration with *vērē* appropriate.)

Have lines 9–11 translated, and ask as before whether the reference is to past, present or future; what is the effect of the first five words of line 9? Question 3 might be taken at this point. Which two lines in lines 1–8 do lines 9–11 correspond to? (If pupils are asked 'How do lines 1–2 *differ* in tone from 9–11?', they may spot the change from the gentle urging of the subjunctives in 1–2 to the brusque imperatives of 9–11.) In which line does Catullus emphasise that he must pull himself together and not weaken?

When lines 12–19 have been translated, establish that the reference is now to the future. Whom has Catullus been addressing in lines 1–11? Whom does he address in lines 12ff.? How will he show the determination he refers to in line 12 (*obdūrat*)? Question 4 might be considered at this point. What question does Catullus repeatedly ask, in varying ways, in lines 16–18, and what answer does he imply to his own question? (Various possibilities might be suggested: 'He doesn't know, but is curious to learn'; 'Nobody'; 'He realistically knows that there *will* be somebody, and that the "somebody" won't be him.') Whom has he been addressing in lines 12–18? Why does he need to switch in line 19 to addressing himself?

Question 5 could now be considered, supplemented if necessary by such questions as 'What feelings make it hard for him to be firm? What feelings help him? Have you met this mixture of feelings in any other Catullus poems?' Question 6 might also lead to a corollary: 'What is Catullus' attitude to Lesbia in lines 15–18? Vindictive, compassionate, cynical, infatuated, or some or none of these?'

Balme and Warman 107–8 have questions comparing this poem with Michael Drayton's sonnet 'Since there's no help, come let us kiss and part'. *Omnibus* 2, pages 19 and 21, contains two translations of 'miser Catulle . . .' by sixth-formers; pupils may like to discuss and compare them, and then perhaps attempt versions of their own, either of this poem or of another in this Stage.

Suggestions for consolidation: future active, passive and deponent (13–18); 3rd person plural perfect in *-ēre* (3, 8).

Vocabulary check: *fulgeō* (3, 8); *quondam* (3); *quō* (4); *fīō* (6); *vīvō* (10); *at* (14, 19); *doleō* (14); *videor* (16).

VIII 'Fūrī et Aurēlī . . . (*Poem* 11)

Lyne discusses the poem helpfully in *Handbook* 30–3 and in Greig 23–8. See also the questions in Balme and Warman (52).

Notes

18 **complexa:** Encourage pupils to move from the literal translation ('having embraced') to more idiomatic versions ('in her embrace', etc.).

24 **postquam:** Note how pupils cope with the postponement of this word, and give help with comprehension questions if necessary.

The following questions may help the class to establish the sense of the passage after the initial reading aloud:

What is Lesbia to do? Who with?
What is she doing? How many?
Truly doing what? But repeatedly doing what?
What does Catullus say she is *not* to do?
When could she have counted on his love?
What has happened to his love? What is it compared to?
What has happened to the flower?

After translation, questions 1 and 2 could be discussed. Some pupils may feel that Furius and Aurelius are being compared favourably with

Lesbia, as truly loyal comrades whom Catullus knows he can rely on; others may feel that the extravagant compliments of lines 1–16 indicate irony, and that Furius and Aurelius are two of Lesbia's current lovers. In studying Catullus' message to Lesbia, the class might be asked to find the pairs of contrasting words in lines 19–20 (*amāns* ... *rumpēns*; *nūllum* ... *omnium*).

In considering question 3, the pupils might note that *identidem* occurs both here and in 'ille mī pār esse ...' (p. 92, line 3) and that the stanzas of both poems consist of three short lines followed by a very short one. (They are in fact the only two surviving poems by Catullus in Sapphic metre, though Lyne argues against attaching significance to this.) *vīvat valeatque* (line 17) might conceivably be echoing *vīvāmus* ... *atque amēmus* (p. 93, line 1). Is this coincidence? Is Catullus recalling past expressions of love in order to strengthen present expressions of rejection?

The simile in lines 21–4 may lead to the question: what are the points of similarity between Catullus' love and the flower? If his love is being compared to the flower, what (if anything) corresponds to the plough? Is it significant that a plough is inanimate ('The agent of destruction ... does not intend or know what it has done', Lyne *Handbook* 33), and that the flower is at the edge of the meadow, killed by a pure fluke?

The contrast of mood between lines 17–20 and 21–4 is variously interpreted. Many commentators take 17–20 as bitter, heartfelt abuse, replaced by a gentler tone in 21–4 as the tender simile gets under way; Lyne, however, reads 17–20 as lively but not too serious ribaldry, and 21–4 as a more earnest, urgent message.

Question 4 invites the class to consider whether lines 17–24 should be taken at face value. Some pupils (and scholars) read the text as a final dismissal of Lesbia (or even as the rejection of an offer of reconciliation made by Lesbia through Furius and Aurelius as intermediaries). Others feel that Catullus 'protests too much', and is using words of dismissal to make a veiled appeal to Lesbia to resume their relationship. Others again see in this poem a recurrence of the *ōdī-et-amō* theme. Lyne, warning against a too ready assumption that the poem marks the final breakdown of the relationship, points out that lovers have a notorious habit of saying goodbye more than once.

This would be a possible point for the class to consider the order in which the poems of Stage 45 have been arranged. Would it have been a more convincing sequence if the poems had been printed in their manuscript order (III–II–VII–VIII–I–IV–V–VI)? This could in turn raise the vexed but intriguing question of the relationship (if any) between Catullus' poetry and the events in his life. Do the poems provide us with any reason for believing that Lesbia existed and that Catullus had a love affair with her? If pupils are tempted to read the text as a transcript of historical reality, on the grounds that it is 'sincere' or 'convincing', it could be pointed out that much convincing love poetry has been written in the context of wholly imaginary relationships (e.g. *Romeo and Juliet*). If, on the other hand, pupils take up a position of complete scepticism, and argue that we know nothing whatever about the historical Catullus and the historical Lesbia, it could be said that the picture emerging from the poems is at any rate coherent and internally consistent, and that there is at least a little external evidence to support it. For example, some scholars (though not all) believe that 'Lesbia' can be identified with a historical woman, known to us from other sources; pupils could at this point be referred to the background material.

Suggestions for consolidation: jussive subjunctive (17, 21); present participles (19, 20, 23).

Vocabulary check: *vīvō* (17); *simul* (18); *teneō* (18); *vērē* (19); *identidem* (19); *praetereō* (23); *tangō* (24); *arātrum* (24).

Manipulation exercises

Exercise 1 Type: vocabulary
Linguistic feature being practised: antonyms

Exercise 2 Type: transformation
Linguistic feature being practised: present subjunctive active and passive, introduced in Stages 36 and 41
Incidental practice: indirect question

Exercise 3 Type: completion
Missing item: gerund
Criterion of choice: sense
Linguistic feature being practised: accusative, genitive and ablative of gerund, introduced in Stages 41 and 43

For further practice, see Language Information section, p. 214, paragraph 1.

Third language note (dative of disadvantage)

This linguistic feature sometimes disconcerts the pupils. They feel that 'advantage' and 'disadvantage' are natural opposites, and that it is illogical of Latin to use the same case for both. Encourage them to look not just at the dative, but at the sentence as a whole, for instance by comparing the example in paragraph 1 with the first example in paragraph 2. Each sentence contains a nominative (*pater*, *Fortūna*) indicating the person or agency who did the action, an accusative (*dōnum*, *frātrem*) indicating the person or thing to whom the action was done, and also a dative (*nōbīs*, *mihi*) indicating another person or persons involved in the action. Whether they gain or lose by this involvement may affect the way the sentence is translated; but it does not affect the relationship of *nōbīs* and *mihi* to the other words in the sentence.

Examples of the dative of disadvantage met earlier in Unit IVB:
1 *fortūna mihī tētē abstulit ipsum.* (Stage 42, p. 34, line 5)
2 *miser indignē frāter adēmpte mihī.* (Stage 42, p. 34, line 6)
3 *fortūna mihi nōn omnia ēripuit.* (Stage 43, p. 61, line 5)
4 *quod omnēs/ēripit sēnsūs mihi.* (Stage 45, p. 92, lines 5–6)
5 *tam bellum mihi passerem abstulistis.* (Stage 45, p. 96, line 15)

The background material

Wiseman 15–53 provides an illuminating and immensely readable account of Clodia Metelli. Her identification with Lesbia is discussed by, amongst others, Austin 148–50 (who regards the identification as 'probable'), Fordyce xiv–xviii ('not unlikely') and Quinn *Catullus* xvi–xviii ('extremely probable'). Wiseman rejects the identification, and is at pains to separate his account of Catullus and Lesbia (130–82) from what he says about Clodia Metelli.

One purpose of this section of background material is to introduce the pupils, however cursorily, to Roman oratory and Cicero, since they are unrepresented elsewhere in Unit IVB. If the class contains effective and confident readers, they should each be asked to read aloud one of the quoted paragraphs to the rest of the class. Pupils should have no difficulty in picking up Cicero's allusions to the rumours about Clodia's incest and the murder of Metellus (bottom line of the translation on p. 110 of the pupil's text, and last paragraph on p. 111); the teacher might mention the ambiguity of *amīca* ('friend' in line 5, p. 111; the word can have either a respectable or disreputable meaning).

The class might also look at translations of one or two Catullus poems which are or might be connected with Clodia, Cicero and Caelius Rufus. In *Poem* 77 Catullus addresses a Rufus with great bitterness, accusing him of breach of friendship and perhaps of stealing his mistress from him; in *Poem* 58 he addresses a Caelius, lamenting the promiscuity and degradation of Lesbia; in Poem 49 he addresses Cicero in complimentary (or mock-complimentary) terms, thanking him effusively for an unspecified favour (believed by some to be the delivery of the *Pro Caelio*; Quinn and Fordyce are both sceptical).

Interpretations of the 4th-century mosaic shown on p. 109 in which the girls are obviously displaying their charms vary considerably and include a water-ballet and an athletic contest, either real or parodied. According to the latter, the top row shows a competitor for the long jump (holding weights), a discus thrower and two runners, and the bottom row the prize-giving, with crowns and victory palms, as well as two girls playing ball.

Suggestions for discussion

1 How fair do Cicero's remarks seem to you? How relevant? Do they give you an unfavourable impression of Roman justice?

2 Is Cicero's description of Clodia consistent with the picture of Lesbia presented by Catullus?

3 Does it 'matter' who Lesbia was? Does it make the poems more enjoyable? more interesting?

Vocabulary checklist

Encourage the class to recall the links between *candidus* and *candidātus* and between *ōtium* and *negōtium*. With the cognates *culpa–culpāre*, compare *cēna–cēnāre*, *cūra–cūrāre*, *lacrima–lacrimāre*, *mora–morārī*, *mina–minārī* and *pugna–pugnāre*. To the compounds of *rumpere* add *interrumpere*, *perrumpere* and *prōrumpere*, and note how the meaning of *corrumpere* shifted to become metaphorical. With *tegō* compare *tēctum*, which the pupils have already met in the sense of 'roof' and are about to meet in the sense of 'building'.

Suggestions for further work

1 If the teacher senses that this Stage has gone down well with the class, pupils could be asked to pick a favourite poem from the selection and write about ten lines on it, saying why it appealed to them.

2 The class may enjoy listening to some of Carl Orff's *Carmina Catulli*, which include 'ille mī pār esse . . .', 'vīvāmus, mea Lesbia . . .', 'lūgēte, ō Venerēs . . .', 'ōdī et amō . . .' and 'miser Catulle . . .', and (in *Carmina Catulli* II) 'multās per gentēs . . .' from Stage 42. How well do they think Orff's melodies and rhythms capture the mood of Catullus?

3 Present the class with copies of two or more translations of one of the poems in this selection for comparative study and discussion.

4 Some of the class may be interested in reading further in the translation of the *Pro Caelio*. If they want to sample another Cicero speech, they might enjoy the narrative portions of the *Pro Cluentio* or (if they want to see Cicero on the side of the prosecution) parts of the *Verrines*.

STAGE 46: CLĀDĒS

Synopsis

Reading passages	Pliny, *Letters* VI.20.2–20 (adapted)
Background material	time-chart (authors)
Language notes	pluperfect subjunctive passive conditional clauses with pluperfect subjunctive omission of forms of *esse*

The reading material in this Stage is taken from Pliny's vivid description of the eruption of Vesuvius in A.D. 79, still quoted by modern vulcanologists as a classic account of a volcanic catastrophe.

Title picture

An eighteenth-century engraving of the eruption of Vesuvius in 1754.

tremōrēs I (*Letters* VI.20.2–8)

The commentaries of Sherwin-White and Levens will be useful throughout this Stage.

The teacher might introduce this letter by reading part of the translation of its companion-piece (VI.16, on the death of the elder Pliny), e.g. paragraphs 4–10, from the first sighting of the volcanic cloud to the departure of Pliny the Elder on his rescue mission. Use the map on p. 116 of the pupil's text to establish the positions of Misenum (base of the western Italian fleet, of which the Elder Pliny was commander), Vesuvius, Pompeii, Herculaneum, Naples and Stabiae (where Pliny the Elder perished).

Notes

3–4 **tremor terrae . . . solitus:** The class may recall the earthquake that shook Pompeii severely in A.D. 63. Its effects are illustrated on p. 117 of the pupil's text.

4 **Campāniae:** A reminder may be necessary that this was the name of the district, not of a particular town.

7 **āreā domūs . . . dīvidēbat:** 'The house [of the Elder Pliny] is within the town of Misenum, and is built by the shore' (Sherwin-White). Only a narrow courtyard separates sea from

house, and so when the buildings begin to shake (lines 13–14) the danger to those in the courtyard is very great.

8–9 **librum . . . legere coepī:** Some details, omitted from this adapted version for the sake of simplicity, could be supplied by the teacher: the book Pliny demanded was a volume of Livy and, following his uncle's usual practice (*Letters* III.5.10), he made notes and extracts from it as he read.

13 **hōra dieī prīma:** The day is 25 August and the hour about 6 a.m.; at such a time and date one would normally expect bright sunshine in Campania, which adds point to Pliny's next remark.

14 **fugere:** i.e. right out of the town, well away from any collapsing buildings. 'They pass along the neck of land to the north of the town [see map], till they reach the ground rising up to the hill beyond Baiae, whence they look down [cf. 'tremōrēs' II, p. 116, line 15] to the promontory and to the island of Capri beyond' (Sherwin-White).

The main focus of attention in this section might be the causes and circumstances of the flight of Pliny and his mother; use the map in the pupil's text, and the notes above where appropriate, to establish a clear picture of the topography in pupils' minds. Detailed discussion of Pliny's behaviour can perhaps best be left to arise from the reading of the next section, but the class might be invited to comment on his sang-froid, as displayed in lines 8–13. Levens (152–3) quotes an amusing eighteenth-century criticism of Pliny, written in the form of an imaginary rebuke from his uncle, and continues: 'there is certainly something irritating in Pliny's complacent account of his own imperturbability. At the same time it must be admitted that in finding an occupation to steady his nerves he was acting very sensibly.'

Some suggested questions

How did Pliny spend the rest of the day after his uncle's departure?

What signs of trouble had been noticed during the previous few days? Why did this cause less panic than might have been expected? How did the situation change during the night?

What did Pliny's mother do when the tremors became violent? What was Pliny himself doing, and with what purpose in mind? What did he and his mother do then?

How did Pliny try to calm his mother's fears? Who was his uncle's friend angry with, and why? What was Pliny's reaction to the friend's rebuke?

Why did Pliny and his mother finally decide to leave? How far did they go before stopping?

For other possible questions, see Tingay *Comprehendite* 47 (to which the present version is indebted for two adaptations of Pliny's original: *ipse* in line 6 for Pliny's *invicem,* and *dubia lūx* in line 13 for *dubius et quasi languidus diēs*).

Suggestions for consolidation: word order of *irrūpit cubiculum meum māter* and *advenit amīcus* (5–6, 9; for further examples, see Appendix B); historic present (9–11, 16–17); *ad* with gerundive (6) and gerund (16); present passive infinitive (5); ablative absolute (1, 13–14).

Vocabulary check: *proficīscor* (1); *ideō* (1); *quia* (4); *videor* (5); *poscō* (8); *ōtium* (9); *quīdam* (9); *etiam* (10); *adhūc* (13); *cōnstituō* (15); *cōnsistō* (16); *patior* (17).

tremōrēs II (*Letters* VI.20.8–12)

Notes

1 **vehicula:** The original plan was to escape from the town on foot, then take to the carriages if it became necessary to flee further. In the event, the plan of using carriages is abandoned, and when Pliny and his mother resume their flight (lines 20–1), they proceed on foot.

3 **mare in sē resorbērī:** perhaps because of disturbance of the sea-bed.

5 **ab alterō latere:** i.e. landward, as opposed to the sea scene just described.

6 **nūbēs ātra:** the cloud of ash and smoke in which Pliny the Elder choked to death at Stabiae. Pompeii and Herculaneum suffered especially severely from this cloud, owing to the strength and direction of the wind (see map on p. 116 of pupil's text).

7 **fulguribus:** Lightning is in fact often generated during a volcanic eruption. It is shown clearly in Turner's painting *Vesuvius in Eruption* (reproduced in, e.g., Feder 11).

8 **vehementius:** cf. *impēnsius*, Stage 45, p. 99, line 5.

15 **Capreās, Misēnī prōmunturium:** Further reference to the map in pupil's text may be helpful.

16 **ōrāre hortārī iubēre:** handled in the pupil's glossary. Historic infinitives are the subject of a language note in Stage 48.

18 **corpore:** Evidently she was somewhat on the stout side, like her brother (Pliny, *Letters* VI.16.13).

Pupils might be allowed to answer question 2 with a drawing. This can and should be as rigorous and demanding a task as a verbal description.

Since the object is to test comprehension, pupils' intentions are more important than draughtsmanship.

The main focus for discussion might be the behaviour of Pliny, his mother and the friend. Encourage variety of opinion in response to question 6. Pliny and his mother could be regarded as courageous or foolhardy, the friend as cowardly or sensible ('We can hardly blame [him] for losing his temper; young Pliny's insufferable priggishness must have been getting on his nerves for some time', Levens 154). There is obvious educational value in encouraging pupils to look critically at the way material is presented in historical sources such as the present text. For example, Pliny's emphasis in lines 13–14 on the speed and direction of the friend's departure invites the reader to condemn the friend for being self-centred; but the information given by Pliny himself could support a more favourable interpretation, that the friend, having lingered as long as possible to try to dissuade Pliny and his mother from risking their lives in vain, gives up in despair and rushes off at top speed, perhaps to a situation where he can be of more use. The extracts from Tacitus in Stage 48 will provide further opportunities for critical study of this kind.

Such discussion can lead to further questions. Does Pliny's behaviour differ in any way from that of his mother, or are they both presented in very similar terms? Do the class find the account of their behaviour credible? Is it to be dismissed as melodramatic self-glorification, or are such details as *cōgō* and *castīgat* (21) convincing? Were Pliny and his mother right to postpone flight for so long? It is easy to criticise them for foolhardiness, but how many people would in fact run away from a dangerous situation if a friend or relative was still thought to be trapped?

The questions in Tingay *Comprehendite* 47 (especially the final one, which asks pupils to pick out details and phrases which help them to visualise the event) will continue to be a useful source of ideas.

The text contains four examples of subordinate clauses in indirect statement (lines 9–10, 17, 18, 21). If the teacher wishes to practise the point further, examples will be found in Language Information, p. 217 of pupil's text and p. 132 below.

The picture on p. 117 of the pupil's text, showing the effects of the Pompeian earthquake in A.D. 62, is from the relief carved on the *larārium* of the banker Caecilius Iucundus, whom pupils will probably recall from the early Stages of the course. This section shows the Vesuvius Gate collapsing and narrowly missing two mules pulling a cart. For further carvings from this relief, see Royal Academy Exhibition Catalogue 16–17, filmstrip (and slide) I.6 and C.S.C.P. *The Roman World*, Unit II, Book 6, 6–7.

Suggestions for consolidation: participle in agreement with unexpressed subject (12, 20); present passive infinitive (1, 3; cf. 'tremōrēs' I, p. 115, line 5); indirect statement with main verb postponed (3; see also Language Information, pp. 209–10 of pupil's text and p. 129 below); 2nd person plural of present tense of deponent verb (10; this could be practised further through a 'substitution' exercise, e.g. by contrasting *cūnctāminī* with *cūnctābiminī* and *cūnctābāminī*, then with *cūnctantur*, *cūnctor*, *cūnctāmur*, *cūnctāris*, etc.).

Vocabulary check: *īdem* (3); *lītus* (4); *et . . . et* (7, 18); *vehementer* (8); *hortor* (8, 16); *moror* (12, 21); *convertō* (12); *cōgō* (21); *pāreō* (21).

First language note (pluperfect subjunctive passive)

Encourage pupils to volunteer their own comments on the way this tense is formed and the way it differs from the pluperfect indicative passive. Ask them to practise the morphology by converting assorted forms of the pluperfect indicative passive into the corresponding subjunctive forms after *cum*, e.g. by turning *laudātī erāmus*, *ductus erās*, *monita erat*, into *cum laudātī essēmus*, *cum ductus essēs*, *cum monita esset*, adding the translation in each case. For further practice, they could work out the Latin for (e.g.) 'when I had been greeted', 'when you (pl.) had been forced', 'when they had spoken', etc., with the aid of the information given under *salūtō*, *cōgō*, *loquor*, etc. in Part III of the Language Information section.

One or two of the examples in the language note would more usually be expressed in Latin by means of a participial phrase. The teacher might compare *cum omnēs servī dīmissī essent* in paragraph 2 with *omnibus servīs dīmissīs*, and *cum multās gemmās adeptī essēmus* in paragraph 4 with *multās gemmās adeptī*.

tenebrae (*Letters* VI.20.13–16, 18–20)

Notes

5 **nox dēnsissima:** not a real night, but daytime darkness. Pupils may recall a comparable scene from the Virgil extract in Stage 42, p. 42.

11 **nusquam iam deōs ūllōs esse:** The rest of Pliny's sentence (omitted from the pupil's text because of linguistic complexity) makes it clear that the crowd thought they were witnessing the fulfilment of the popular belief that the world's end would be accomplished by a violent conflagration. It was thought that this destruction of the universe would be preceded by the death or departure of the gods.

15–16 **opertī atque etiam oblīsī pondere:** Compare the fate of Pompeii.

18 **diēs rediit:** still 25 August, since the *nox* of lines 5ff. was 'darkness by day'.

20 **noctem:** 25–26 August.

22 **cognōscerēmus . . . esset:** His body was in fact found on the same day, 26 August (*Letters* VI.16.20), but Pliny and his mother may have had to wait some time for news to reach them at Misenum from Stabiae.

Some suggested questions

Why did Pliny and his mother turn aside in their flight? What happened as soon as they had sat down?

What sounds did they hear?

Why were they not reassured when light reappeared in line 12?

What new danger threatened them in lines 14–16? What preventive measures did they take?

When the sun finally appeared in line 18, why were they amazed by what they saw?

Why were they unwilling to leave Misenum again, even though the tremors persisted?

Discussion of this section might concentrate on Pliny's narrative technique, especially in lines 1–11, through such questions as the following:

How effective is the simile in lines 2–3? In what way(s) did the thick black cloud resemble a river?

Does *vix . . . cum* (line 5) merely indicate the time when the two events happened? Or does it emphasise that Pliny and his mother had a narrow escape?

Does the comparison in lines 5–6 help you to imagine the darkness? (In the full text, Pliny contrasts the darkness of a closed unlit room with the less intense darkness of a moonless or cloudy night.)

In each of the two clauses *vōcibus . . . requīrēbant* and *vōcibus . . . nōscitābant*, do the voices belong to the searchers or to the people they are looking for? How detailed a picture does Pliny convey by these four words? Describe the scene in your own words.

Can you find other examples of sentences in which a key word is repeated, in either the same case or a different one? How effective is the paradox *metū mortis mortem precābantur* (9–10)? Is it just a flashy attempt to achieve an impressive phrase, or is it possible that people might indeed, in the agony of suspense, have prayed for what they feared?

Compare the three similes in the passage (lines 2–3, 5–6, 19). Which is the most effective?

Lines 1–11 are very suitable for pupils to read aloud (after a little practice) to the rest of the class, aiming less at melodrama than at an intelligently phrased reading that emphasises the sense of the words. The teacher might round off the story by reading from a translation of Pliny VI.16; if paragraphs 4–10 were read before, paragraphs 11–20 (taking the story down to the discovery of Pliny the Elder's corpse) could be read now.

The pupils' previous encounter with Pliny might be recalled from Stage 41. Do they detect any similarities of character between seventeen-year-old Pliny amidst the eruption, and middle-aged Pliny governing Bithynia?

The photograph of plaster casts of corpses from Pompeii (p. 120) should serve as a reminder that many victims were less successful than Pliny and his mother in avoiding the catastrophic effects of the eruption. Pupils may be able to recall, from their earlier reading about Pompeii, the way in which archaeologists make such casts (see Unit I, Stage 12, p. 15, for details).

Suggestions for consolidation: jussive subjunctive (3; see also Language Information, p. 208 of pupil's text); substantival participle (4; see also Language Information, p. 211 of pupil's text and p. 130 below); 1st person plural of passive (4; cf. *patimur*, 'tremōrēs' I, p. 115, line 17 and *cōnārēmur*, 'tremōrēs' II, p. 116, line 8); purpose clause with *nē* (3–4); possessive dative (21; see also Language Information, p. 205 of pupil's text); omission of first of two verbs (9, 12); conditional sentence with *nisi* (14–15); *attonitī* predicative (18; for further examples, see Appendix B); 4th declension (7, 9, 10, 20); genitive of gerund (21; cf. *praecepta volandī*, Stage 44, p. 76, line 6).

Vocabulary check: *quasi* (2, 5); *effundō* (3); *lūmen* (6); *adsum* (6); *requīrō* (8); *cāsus* (9); *lūgeō* (9); *procul* (13); *identidem* (14); *fulgeō* (18); *mūtō* (19); *abeō* (21); *cognōscō* (22).

Second language note (conditional clauses with pluperfect subjunctive)

For further practice, examples already met in the reading material can be picked out and retranslated. For instance:

ego ipse . . . efficere potuissem. (Stage 43, p. 58, lines 5–6)
sī precibus . . . ultrā cupīvissēmus? (Stage 43, p. 60, lines 3–4)
sī diūtius . . . periissēmus. (Stage 46, p. 115, lines 15–16)

sī adfuissēs . . . fēminārum. (Stage 46, p. 120, lines 6–7)
nisi identidem . . . pondere essēmus. (Stage 46, p. 120, lines 14–16)

Ask the class 'Does the first example in paragraph 1 imply that the young man *did* look round?' 'Does the first example in paragraph 2 imply that the sailors *did* remain in port?', etc., to establish that in each of these sentences the condition is an 'impossible' one, incapable of being fulfilled.

Manipulation exercises and further practice

Exercise 1 Type: transformation
Linguistic features being practised: singular and plural of nouns and adjectives

If pupils have difficulty with the absence of an expressed subject in sentence 7, or the ablative of comparison in sentence 8, discussion and further practice may be appropriate. Explanation and practice are also sometimes required in connection with *tuī* and *meīs* in sentences 2 and 8; some pupils try to change them to forms of *vester* and *noster*, or are misled by the idea of 'possession' into attempting to turn *meīs* into the genitive.

Exercise 2 Type: translation from English, based on 'tremōrēs' I, p. 115, lines 1–12
Linguistic features being practised: various forms of verb and noun

Translation from English into Latin has occurred in the Course so far only in the form of suggested substitution drills ('If *parābant* means "they were preparing", what's the Latin for "we were preparing"?', etc.) or guided composition such as Stage 43 exercise 3. The present exercise is somewhat more advanced (but note that all the vocabulary and much of the morphology is given in the original passage). The pupils could do some or all of the sentences working together as a class, with one pupil writing up the Latin translation on the blackboard. Alternatively, pupils might work in groups; each group could then mark another group's work. If the teacher makes up further sentences on similar lines using this or other passages in Unit IVB, it will usually be found advisable to go cautiously and not require the class to execute too many changes from the original text.

Exercise 3 Type: substitution
Linguistic feature being practised: connecting relative, introduced in Unit IIIA

This is the last and most difficult of a series of substitution exercises involving *is* (Stage 24 exercise 2) and *quī* (Stage 35 exercise 3, Stage 40 exercise 3). The difficulty can be very much lessened if the teacher first elicits from the class that the case of the relative pronoun will always be the same as the case of the noun it is replacing.

This Stage would be a suitable point to begin consolidation work based on the 'Accidence' and 'Syntax' sections of the Language Information material; see pp. 127–32 below for commentary.

Third language note (omission of forms of esse)

Demonstrate to the class that this linguistic feature, far from being an eccentric peculiarity of Latin, is already very familiar to them in English, e.g. in colloquialisms ('No problem', 'Pity you didn't say so'), school reports ('A recent improvement'), written messages ('Supper in oven'), newspaper headlines ('Two climbers missing') and Mr. Micawber ('Annual income twenty pounds, annual expenditure nineteen nineteen six, result happiness. Annual income twenty pounds, annual expenditure twenty pounds ought and six, result misery'). Encourage pupils to suggest further examples.

The background material

The information presented in the time-chart has been deliberately kept brief; experience shows that multiplicity of detail often leads pupils to forget or muddle more important points. After they have studied the chart, an effective way of testing and reinforcing their grasp of the information is to list authors and works in two columns on the blackboard, in scrambled order, e.g.:

Ovid	epigrams	
Pliny	*Aeneid*	
Virgil	speeches	
Tacitus	the 'Lesbia' poems	etc.

With their textbooks closed, pupils then have to match each author with the correct work.

Encourage pupils to contribute further information about any of these authors from their own knowledge, and to recall (from the Stage 42 time-chart or elsewhere) any ways in which the various authors are connected either with each other or with some particular event or imperial reign. For example, the possible link between Catullus and Cicero, through Clodia and Caelius Rufus, might be recalled from the background material of Stage 45; the class could be reminded that both these authors were writing during the last years of the Republic, and may remember that they were also contemporaries of Julius Caesar, who featured prominently in the Stage 42 time-chart and whose exploits in Britain and Gaul were referred to by Catullus in his poem 'Fūrī et Aurēlī ...' (p. 104 of pupil's text). Virgil and Ovid, on the other hand, lived in the era of civil war and the establishment of the principate by Augustus; the class may recall from the background material of Stage 39 that Augustus punished Ovid and was a patron of Virgil. Similarly, the teacher might remind the class of the links between Petronius and Nero, Pliny and Tacitus (who received Pliny's letter about the eruption of Vesuvius on which the Latin passages in this Stage are based), Pliny and Trajan (Stage 41), Tacitus and Agricola (Stage 26), and Martial and Domitian (Stage 36). Discussion of this sort can be very helpful in drawing together a number of rather scattered threads and giving the pupils as coherent a picture as possible of the chronology of the various authors and their historical context. The teacher may wish to give special emphasis to Virgil and Tacitus, from whose work the passages in Stages 47 and 48 are taken.

Vocabulary checklist

The different forms of *sternō* may require comment from the teacher and special attention from the pupils; with *strātus* compare 'prostrate'. With the cognates *iūdex–iūdicāre* compare *rēx–regere*, *dux–dūcere* and *lūx–lūcēre*; with *iūdicāre–iūdicium* compare *aedificāre–aedificium*, *imperāre–imperium*, *bene + facere–beneficium*, *studēre–studium*, *gaudēre–gaudium*, *taedet–taedium*, and *coniungere–coniugium*.

Suggestions for further work

1 Ask the class to write a summary, in not more than (e.g.) 150 or 200 words, of the events described in the Latin passages in this Stage (an extremely difficult exercise, but very good for testing comprehension).

2 Read Samuel Pepys' eye-witness description of the great fire of London (*Diary* 2 September 1666) and ask the class to compare it with Pliny's account of the Vesuvius eruption. What similarities and differences do they notice in (a) subject-matter (b) manner of telling the story?

3 This Stage provides a convenient opportunity to recall details of the destruction and excavation of Pompeii. To prompt pupils' memory, a selection of frames from Filmstrip 1 (or slides from the first edition of Unit I) might be shown, and the class be asked to provide identification, comment, etc. as appropriate. They are often pleased to discover how much they can remember from the early Stages of the course.

STAGE 47: LŪDĪ

Synopsis

Reading passages	(from) Virgil, *Aeneid* V.114–243 (part Latin, part translation)
Background material	Homer's chariot-race (*Iliad* XXIII.358–441, 499–533, in translation)
Language notes	ablative meaning 'in' or 'from' without preposition plural for singular

Virgil's narrative of the boat-race, with its vivid incidents and sympathetically observed characters, is a virtually self-contained episode, leading up gradually to a natural climax in the moment of victory. In order to give pupils as complete a view as possible of the episode while keeping the Latin text to a length that they can comfortably manage at this stage, the story is told partly in the original and partly in translation, with occasional abridgement. To illustrate the way in which Virgil (like other Roman poets) made creative use of Greek predecessors, a translation of Homer's chariot-race is included as background material for comparison with Virgil's boat-race.

certāmen I (*Aeneid* V.114–23, in translation, abridged)

The commentaries of R. D. Williams (large commentary on *Aeneid* V, shorter notes in his commentary on *Aeneid* I–VI), and of Page, will be helpful throughout this Stage.

The class might begin by recalling the reason for the Trojans' wanderings, and their quest for a new home. Then the translated passage could be read aloud, by teacher or pupil.

The ships are of different sizes but have equal numbers of rowers. Each ship is named after a monster, which would be represented by the ship's figurehead; Pristis (possibly a sawfish) is unlikely to be known to pupils, but they may have come across Scylla, centaurs or the fire-breathing Chimaera in classical studies courses or elsewhere. The names of the four captains and their ships might be written up in two columns in a corner of the blackboard, or on an overhead projector (O.P.) transparency, perhaps with the addition of Gyas' helmsman Menoetes, then kept for reference during the reading of the episode. The class may also be helped by a blackboard diagram (or further O.P.

transparencies), on which the positions of the four ships are marked and then altered as the race proceeds.

The teacher may wish to revise some words that the class have met previously but may well have forgotten and which occur in this Stage, e.g.: *aequor*, *aethēr*, *lītus*, *pelagus*, *saxum*, *sīdus*, *unda*; *cursus*, *mēta*, *pondus*, *rēmus*; etc. When revising these words, help the class by supplying a context; thus, not 'What does *mēta* mean?' or 'What are *rēmī*?' but 'The ships had to race to a *mēta* and back; what was a *mēta*?' or 'What were the *rēmī* which the sailors used?' The Latin words, perhaps with their English translations, can be written up on the board during the course of the revision.

certāmen II (*Aeneid* V.124–7, 129–31, 139–41, 151–8)

Virgil presents the learner with special problems as well as special rewards, and even when comprehension of his words is relatively easy, he can be an exceptionally difficult poet to translate. It will normally be advisable for the teacher to precede translation with plenty of comprehension questions. Some of the questions printed in the pupil's text, e.g. on the present passage and on 'victor' II, could be set as homework, for pupils to answer in writing during their first exploration of the passage, proceeding to translation after their answers have been gone over in class. Since Virgil provides particularly rich opportunities for discussing the nuances of translation, the teacher might sometimes pick a short passage for corporate translation by teacher and class working together, with the final version written up on the blackboard.

Notes

2 **summersum tunditur:** Encourage pupils to translate the participle and verb with two finite verbs ('is submerged and battered', etc.).

6 **signum:** predicative. The first parts of question 2 may help.

6–7 **unde revertī scīrent:** The purpose clause dependent on *unde*, and the infinitive dependent on *scīrent*, are likely to cause trouble. Use comprehension questions to establish the sense before eliciting a translation. Williams has: 'so that they should know where to make the turn for home'.

7 **ubi:** postponed. Compare the previous example in line 3, which is explained in the glossary.

12 **Gyās:** If the long postponement of the subject causes difficulty, try a simpler example, e.g. *appāruit in līmine nūntius*; but also

encourage comment on the effect produced by the word order (see above, foot of p. 4).

15 **priōrem:** not the overall lead, but a lead in the struggle for third place.

16 **victam:** perfect passive participle in accusative. For further examples, see Appendix B.

18 **longā . . . vada salsa carīnā:** If the class are encouraged to listen carefully when the teacher reads the line aloud, they will find it easier to disentangle the two noun + adjective phrases.

Discussion might begin with Virgil's description of the rock. He pictures it in both calm and stormy weather, and each description involves both sound and appearance. The class might be asked what use Virgil makes of contrasting words or phrases to emphasise the difference between the two descriptions. Which words or phrases in line 4 correspond to *tumidīs . . . flūctibus* (lines 2–3), *tunditur* (line 2) and *summersum* (line 2)? (The picture in the pupil's text may be helpful here.)

It may be necessary to emphasise to the class that the course the contestants are to follow is a double one, out to the rock, round it and back again, in the manner of a chariot-race. They might be asked what the purpose of the oak-branch is.

Pupils might try their wits on one puzzle mentioned by Williams: why is Cloanthus said (in lines 13–14) to be held back by the weight of his ship, whereas earlier it was Gyas whose ship was mentioned as especially massive? The gloss on *iūnctīs* (line 15) could be compared with the word's literal translation: what does the literal meaning suggest about the appearance of the two prows? Finally, the class might consider the questions 'Which lines are most easily visualised? At what points can we hear as well as see the action?'

Suggestions for consolidation: 3rd person plural perfect in *-ēre* (9; the examples in the Language Information section, p. 189 of the pupil's text, might be studied at this point; more examples will be met in this Stage and more again in Stage 48); split phrases (3, 5, 7, etc.; for further examples, see Appendix B).

Vocabulary check: *procul* (1); *pelagus* (1); *lītus* (2); *sīdus* (3); *revertor* (6); *aethēr* (9); *unda* (11); *cōnsequor* (13); *rēmus* (13); *pondus* (13); *praetereō* (16); *ūnā* (17).

Gyās et Cloanthus I (*Aeneid* V.159–71 in translation)

When the passage has been read, check that the class have a clear grasp of the situation, especially the point of Gyas' instructions in line 5 and the reason why Cloanthus is able to overtake him. A blackboard diagram is helpful at this point (note that the boats go round the rock anti-clockwise). The need for careful judgement at the turn, going neither too close nor too wide, could be compared with the tactics necessary in chariot-racing.

What impression of Gyas' character do the class have from this extract?

Gyās et Cloanthus II (*Aeneid* V.172–3, 175–82)

The questions in the pupil's text are intended for use *after* the passage has been read and the surface meaning established. The teacher will probably need to give plenty of help on first reading, for example by simple comprehension questions ('What feeling blazed up? Where?' etc.).

Notes

1 **iuvenī:** pupils are initially likely to translate as 'of the young man'; the teacher might accept this translation but return to the word when the whole passage has been read and discuss the case further.
ossibus: The context will probably suggest an appropriate rendering ('in the bones', etc.); local ablatives are discussed in the next language note.

4 **rēctor . . . magister:** both words predicative. Question 2 may help.

6 **ut:** postponed. Pupils often overlook it.
fundō . . . īmō: Note how the class copes with this noun + adjective phrase; if they are baffled, ask them whether there is an adjective describing *fundō* anywhere in the line.

9 **et . . . et:** Compare a simpler example if necessary, e.g. *et rēgēs et urbēs* from Stage 45, p. 92, lines 15–16.

10 **pectore:** The context gives a strong clue to the meaning of the ablative; further examples will follow in the next language note.
salsōs . . . flūctūs: The phrase might be specially drawn to the pupils' attention; they will meet it again in the middle of a difficult sentence in 'victor' II. For suggestions on handling the separation of noun and adjective, see above on *fundō . . . īmō*, line 6.

Some suggested questions

Is 'sadness' a good translation for *dolor* (line 1)? If not, can you suggest an improvement?

Can you recall another poem in which emotion was, as in line 1, felt in the bones or limbs? (If the class are reminded that in the previous poem the feeling was described as a *tenuis flamma* this may help them recall Catullus' description from Stage 45 (p. 92, lines 9–10).)

Does *altā* (line 3) add anything important to your impression of the scene?

What translation would you suggest for *gravis* (line 6)? (Page has 'heavily', Williams 'in his sorry state'. The point might be made that this is a problem purely for the translator, not for the reader or listener; Virgil's original audience could have responded to several different associations of *gravis* simultaneously, without feeling any need to choose between them.)

Is the behaviour of Gyas and Menoetes appropriate to their respective ages? If Gyas' action is grossly stupid, does *iuvenis* (line 1) imply an excuse for him?

Do you agree with Page's comment on the Trojans' mirth in lines 9–10, 'Such merriment is natural, but we could spare the description of it in poetry'?

Question 6 might be used to bring out the point that Virgil presents the episode to us both through the eyes of the spectators (in the description of Menoetes' actions) and from his own point of view through 'editorial' comments such as *gravis*, *iam senior*, etc.

Suggestions for consolidation: verb + nominative word order (1, 2; for further examples, see Appendix B); accusative + nominative + verb word order (9; see Appendix B); 3rd person plural perfect in *-ēre* (2, 9; the class might note that *rīsēre* is used side by side with historic present *rīdent* in 10); split phrases (1, 3, etc.).

Vocabulary check: *cāreō* (2); *hortor* (5); *lītus* (5); *at* (6); *flūctus* (10).

Sergestus et Mnēstheus I (*Aeneid* V.183–200 in translation)

Virgil now switches from the struggle for first place to the battle between the third and fourth boats. Remind the class of the description of the two prows at the end of 'certāmen' II, and use a diagram to establish the positions of Sergestus and Mnestheus; Sergestus is in front, on the inside. Line 6 may need explanation: Mnestheus is striding up and down a central gangway.

The pupils might consider why Mnestheus mentions Hector and the crew's previous adventures in his pep-talk (lines 8–11), and how the sentence might have ended that breaks off at 'perhaps' (line 13); has Mnestheus accepted loss of first prize as inevitable, or does he still nourish a secret hope? Does he attract the reader's sympathy (Williams contrasts the tone of Mnestheus' speech with the previous arrogance and brutality of Gyas)?

Sergestus et Mnēstheus II (*Aeneid* V.201–4, 207–9)

The teacher might first take the class through the glossary and read the passage aloud to them, then ask the following questions, to be answered in writing and marked on the spot by the pupils:

What did chance do?
What was Sergestus doing in line 2? in line 3?
What happened to him?
What did the sailors do?
What did they bring out? What do you think their reason was?
What did they gather up? Where from?

When the answers have been marked and the passage read aloud again, the class can proceed to translation. The main points of difficulty will probably be the interlacing of the noun + adjective phrases in line 1, the postponement of *dum* in line 2, and the use of *īnfēlīx* to refer to Sergestus in line 4.

Establish that *honōrem* (line 1) refers to success in the race, and that *optātum* refers back to Mnestheus' words in Part I; then encourage pupils to explain in their own words the situation described in lines 2–3. Sergestus is afraid that if he goes too wide Mnestheus will cut in behind him and overtake on the inside (as Cloanthus did to Gyas earlier); he tries to pre-empt this by steering into the danger area (*spatiō . . . inīquō*, line 3) close to the turn, but fouls his boat on the reef which projects outwards (*prōcurrentibus*, line 4) from the rock, mostly or wholly under water. Virgil attributes the crash to *ipse . . . cāsus* (line 1); do pupils feel that any word or phrase in lines 2 and 3 suggests a different cause?

Line 4 might be read aloud, and contrasted with a more dactylic line (such as line 8 or 9 in 'certāmen' II, p. 130); the class could then be asked if the sound of the line is in any way suited to the sense. They might also consider whether 'Up jump the sailors' or 'The sailors jump up' more faithfully renders the start of line 5; questions like this help pupils to see that a Latin author's variation of word order is not merely random or wilful.

The meaning of *magnō clāmōre morantur* (line 5) is disputed. The glossary follows Williams in interpreting it as 'hold the ship steady while shouting loudly'. Most other commentators say 'shout loudly at the delay'. Which explanation do the class prefer? Which suits the situation better? The class might also consider the shouts; do they imagine these are shouts of panic? despair at the crew's ruined prospects in the race?

The relief from an Attic inscription shown on p. 135 of the pupil's text gives names of archons (magistrates) for the year A.D. 164–5. There were boat-races, some between triremes, at various festivals in Athens, and this boat is probably a trireme tender, a small boat used for ferrying stores, oarsmen, etc. to and from the trireme. The number of oarsmen is determined by artistic rather than factual considerations.

Suggestions for consolidation: *interior* predicative (3; see Appendix B).

Vocabulary check: *optō* (1); *īnfēlīx* (4); *haereō* (4); *frangō* (7).

First language note (ablative meaning 'in' or 'from' without preposition)

Pupils are sometimes dismayed by the apparently limitless range of possible meanings for the ablative, but reassured by a demonstration that the context normally makes the required meaning clear. The teacher might pick out a number of examples already met in Unit IVB, in which the ablative means 'in', 'from', 'with', 'than', etc.; after a reminder of the context, the class could be asked to identify the ablative and translate the sentence, noting how the appropriate translation of the ablative is determined by the rest of the sentence. Possible examples include:

quid magis est saxō dūrum? (Stage 42, p. 40, line 7)
errāmus pelagō. (Stage 42, p. 42, line 13)
flāvam . . . pollice cēram mollībat. (Stage 44, p. 74, lines 6–7)
quā tē regiōne requīram? (Stage 44, p. 81, line 13)
quem plūs illa oculīs suīs amābat (Stage 45, p. 96, line 5)
sed obstinātā mente perfer, obdūrā. (Stage 45, p. 102, line 11)
tranquillō silet. (Stage 47, p. 129, line 4)
prīmīsque ēlābitur undīs (Stage 47, p. 130, line 11)
exarsit . . . dolor ossibus ingēns. (Stage 47, p. 132, line 1)
et salsōs rīdent revomentem pectore flūctūs. (Stage 47, p. 132, line 10)

victor I (*Aeneid* V.210, 212, 220–4)

The comprehension questions in the pupil's text could perhaps be answered on first reading by abler pupils; alternatively, they can be preceded or replaced with such questions as the following:

Which two adjectives in line 1 describe Mnestheus?

Which two verbs in line 2 tell you what he did?
Translate lines 1–2.
Find three present participles in lines 3–5 which describe what Sergestus is doing. Where is he struggling (guide pupils to *brevibus . . . vadīs*, line 4, as well as *in scopulō . . . altō*, line 3)?
Look again at lines 3–5: what does Mnestheus do to Sergestus?
Translate lines 3–5.
Whom and what does Mnestheus now overtake? How is he able to do this?
Translate lines 6–7.

The answer to question 3 in the pupil's text could lead to a recapitulation of the earlier incident involving Gyas and Menoetes.

One or two words might be singled out for study and discussion. For example:

prōna (line 2). Williams points out that two meanings are involved: 'downward', i.e. 'shoreward' (cf. *dē* in *dēcurrit*, and contrast the English expression 'the *high* seas'), and 'easy' (because this is the home stretch, from the rock to the finish, with no awkward turns or obstacles en route).

altō (line 3). The word might at first seem to contradict the earlier description of the rock in 'certāmen' II (p. 129), where it was said to be so low that it became submerged in stormy weather; but, as Williams points out, even a jutting reef is high by comparison with the water around it (as Sergestus has found to his cost).

discentem (line 5). Why not *cōnantem*? What does *discentem* suggest about Sergestus' problem and his efforts to solve it? Is the phrase *frāctīs discentem currere rēmīs* a sympathetic one (Williams quotes Day Lewis, 'taking a lesson in rowing with broken oars', saying it well renders the derisive humour)?

currere (line 5). The class have met this verb many times as 'run', in Stage 44 as 'fly' (p. 76, line 1) and here as 'sail'. What do the three ideas all have in common? What does Virgil gain by using *currere* here rather than a 'normal' word for 'sail'?

Suggestions for consolidation: split phrases (e.g. 2, 3, 5; see also Appendix B).

Vocabulary check: *petō* (2); *pelagus* (2); *discō* (5); *inde* (6); *cēdō* (7).

victor II (*Aeneid* V.225–43)

Notes

1 **iamque:** postponed. Note how the pupils cope, and give help if necessary.

2 **petit:** sc. *Mnēstheus*.

3 **sequentem:** substantival, or in agreement with unexpressed *eum* or *Mnēsthea*.

9 **Cloanthus:** nominative noun placed late in clause. Encourage the class to read the line right through, and if necessary ask them which contestant took the initiative. They may need a reminder of the meaning of *nī* (met in line 6) and a recapitulation of the substance of line 8, in order to see how the long conditional clause of lines 9–10 fits into the sentence as a whole.

10 **-que ... -que:** cf. 'Gyās et Cloanthus' II, p. 132, line 5.

11 **quibus:** possessive dative. Cf. *est mihi magna vīlla*, or *est mihi summum imperium*, etc.

12–13 **vōbīs ... reus:** a very tricky sentence. A good class might be asked to study it in pairs, with a warning about the interlaced noun + adjective phrases; otherwise, help pupils through it with comprehension questions. They may recall the required meaning of *cōnstituō* if reminded that Aeneas *viridem mētam ... cōnstituit* on the rock at the start of the race. Williams has a helpful note on *vōtī reus*, 'bound by the obligation to pay what one has promised'; cf. the related phrase *vōtum solvere* which the class may have come across in dedicatory inscriptions, and which appeared in Stage 44, p. 84, exercise 1.

15 **dīxit:** cf. Stage 44, p. 72, line 6.

16–17 **Nēreidem ... Portūnus:** Pupils might like to identify the characters in the picture on p. 139.

17 **euntem:** cf. *sequentem* in line 3 above.

18 **citius:** The teacher might recall (with a reminder of the context) *impēnsius* (Stage 45, p. 99, line 5) or *vehementius* (Stage 46, p. 116, line 8). Cf. also *melius*.

19 **portū ... altō:** Note how pupils cope with this phrase, after the recent language note on local ablatives.

Questions A1–A4 should help the class to grasp the situation. Mnestheus is gaining on Cloanthus, but is running out of time in which to catch him; his spirited effort to come from behind and overtake the leader in a last-minute spurt wins the hearts of the spectators, who cheer him on enthusiastically. (Do pupils feel Virgil's *cūnctī*, line 3, should be taken literally, or would Cloanthus continue to receive the cheers and encouragement of his own supporters?) Tension in Cloanthus' boat is acute; having led throughout the second half of the race, his crew feel an eleventh-hour defeat would be unbearable, and are straining desperately to hold off their challenger. Mnestheus' men, on the other hand, who were earlier struggling to avoid last place, now find themselves with an outside chance of outright victory. As line 7 makes clear, their success against Sergestus and Gyas has transformed their morale.

The answer to question A5 is disputable; most commentators take line 8 as meaning that the race would have ended in a dead heat, but Williams interprets it as 'having (first) come up level, they would have (gone on and) won the prize'; which interpretation do pupils prefer? As a follow-up to question A6, the class might be asked why Cloanthus chooses these particular deities, or why his promised offerings will be made on the shore and into the sea. Question A8 can be approached by asking pupils to read lines 17–18 aloud. The class could also be asked whether they take *manū magnā . . . impulit* literally or metaphorically; if it is metaphorical, what is happening literally? Question A9 might lead to the further question: which is the more appropriate simile for Cloanthus' boat in line 19, the wind or the arrow?

Harris (*Sport* 128–32; see also his lecture in *Meminisse Iuvabit* 108–10) has an engaging commentary on the race, complete with a detailed diagram (through the class and teacher will probably prefer to work out a diagram for themselves). He is very scathing about Virgil's climax, on the grounds that Cloanthus wins only by cheating – a view which may already have occurred to some members of the class. It is worth discussing the significance and appropriateness of Cloanthus' appeal to the gods. For example, can the intervention of Portunus be given a rationalised interpretation ('inspiration', 'superhuman effort', 'unexpected reserves of strength', etc.)?

Question B1 could be preceded by a retrospective look at the whole race. The class might be required to recapitulate the main events, or the teacher might rapidly retranslate the entire episode, calling on pupils from time to time to supply the translation of individual words or phrases. Williams' view of the four captains is given on pp. xiv–xv of his edition of Book V, and in his note on lines 116f. in his edition of Books I–VI. (Other views are possible, of course. It might be argued that the personalities of the four captains fail to make a lasting impression on the reader; Virgil himself seems to have forgotten the name of the winner by line 493 of Book V.)

When discussing question B2, pupils should be encouraged to demonstrate how they think a particular line or passage ought to be read. (They will find Cloanthus' prayer hard to read accurately because of its unusually large number of elisions; the teacher should not press the class too hard on this.) This could develop into a full-scale reading of the whole Stage (see p. 6 above). To what extent the scansion of the hexameter should be explained depends on the skill and interest of the pupils. Encourage them to 'linger' over syllables that contain long vowels or are succeeded by two consonants; some could go further and work out the scansion in feet – but it would be a pity if over-emphasis on this point led pupils to disregard the words' sense. Dissuade them from trying to read every line in a single breath; indicate that the sense of the words often makes a pause in mid-line appropriate.

Suggestions for consolidation: substantival participle (3, 17); verb + nominative word order (3, 15–16; see also Appendix B); accusative + nominative + verb word order (7; see also Appendix B); conditional sentence with *nisi* (*nī*) and pluperfect subjunctive (8); possessive dative (11; see also Language Information, p. 205 of pupil's text and p. 128 below); ablative of comparison (18; see also Language Information, p. 205 of pupil's text and p. 128 below).

Vocabulary check: *petō* (2); *vīrēs* (2); *aethĕr* (4); *quia* (7); *uterque* (9); *imperium* (11); *aequor* (11); *lītus* (12); *āra* (13); *flūctus* (14, 15); *fundō* (14).

Second language note (plural for singular)

The quotations in paragraph 1 are from Ovid (Stage 44, p. 81, lines 10–11), Virgil (*Aeneid* II.255, IV.646), Wordsworth (*The Solitary Reaper*) and Keats (*On First Looking into Chapman's Homer*). The comparison with English verse may help to make the point that the use of plural for singular is not an odd vagary peculiar to Roman authors, nor is it adopted merely for the sake of the metre (though metrical advantage is often one of its side-effects), but is one of the ways in which poets may choose to express themselves differently from prose writers; other ways include the use of metre, or of a specialised vocabulary (*ēnsis* for *gladius*, 'steed' for 'horse', etc.). English examples of the reverse practice, where the singular is used for the plural ('life on the ocean wave', 'with downcast eye', etc.) might also be quoted.

Williams, on *Aeneid* V.98 (in his large commentary), has a very full and clear account of 'poetic plurals', demonstrating their metrical convenience, distinguishing a number of ways in which their use developed, and recording some interesting objections by ancient critics (including Caesar).

Manipulation exercises

Exercise 1 Type: vocabulary
Linguistic feature being practised: synonyms

Exercise 2 Type: completion
Missing item: verb
Criterion of choice: sense
Linguistic feature being practised: conditional clauses with pluperfect subjunctive, introduced in Stage 46

Exercise 3 Type: substitution
Linguistic feature being practised: deponent verbs
A wide range of morphology is practised, including both present-stem and perfect-stem forms, and a subjunctive in sentence 6. It will usually be advisable to have one or two sentences done orally in class before setting the exercise as written work. Some of the practice exercises on deponent verbs, on pp. 196–7 of the Language Information section, could be used as either a lead-in or a follow-up to this exercise.

Exercise 4 Type: completion
Missing item: noun *or* verb *or* participle *or* adverb
Criterion of choice: sense and syntax, based on Stage 47 reading passages
Linguistic feature being practised: sentence structure

The background material

The lines translated are *Iliad* XXIII.358–60, 362–7, 369–441, 499–516, 523–7, 532–3. It is worth taking some trouble initially to sort out the identity of the chief characters, using the information in the pupil's text and perhaps listing the four contestants on the blackboard. Pupils could read the passage through for themselves as homework; then all or part of it should be read aloud in class. The phrase 'single-foot horses' (horses with single, i.e. uncloven, hooves) may need to be explained.

'The *Aeneid* is a poem wholly different in character from the Homeric poems. Yet it recalls them on every page and is constructed largely by the remoulding of Homeric materials' (Camps 75; see also ibid. 9–10). The gods are involved both in Homer's chariot-race and in Virgil's boat-race, but in very different ways. Portunus' helping hand, which enables Cloanthus to beat Mnestheus to the finishing-line, contrasts sharply with the energetic intervention of Homer's Athene, who not only picks up Diomedes' whip for him but wrecks his rival's chariot in a spectacular smash. Pupils may perhaps notice the further detail that whereas Athene's action is prompted simply by pity for Diomedes, Portunus' intervention is a response to a prayer.

Virgil's imaginative exploitation of Homer can also be illustrated, in microcosm, by a comparison between the incident at the 'narrow place' in Homer's chariot-race and Virgil's two incidents at the rock. In Virgil, the incidents happen at the turning-point; in Homer, the reader *expects* drama at the turn (especially after the long speech of Nestor, not included in the pupil's text, in which he gives Antilochus lengthy advice about rounding the turning-point) but during the race the turn goes unmentioned and the actual drama takes place elsewhere. In Homer, Antilochus refuses to give way in the narrow place, and Menelaus has to drop back or be forced off the road; Virgil reshapes this event and splits it into two complementary incidents, in which first Gyas' helmsman allows himself to be overtaken through taking the turn too wide, and then Sergestus steers too close to the rock and runs aground.

Antilochus' speech to his horses in 44–57 might be compared with Mnestheus' address to his crew in 'Sergestus et Mnēstheus' I, p. 134. In each case, the speaker abandons hope of victory but is desperate to avoid the humiliation of last (or nearly last) place. The tone of the two speeches, however, is utterly different; Mnestheus' appeal is an engaging mixture of passion and humility, whereas Antilochus is all threat and bluster. The pupils will probably be able to find further parallels themselves between Virgil's boat-race and Homer's chariot-race, including some close similarities of verbal detail, e.g. between line 8 of 'victor' II, p. 138, and lines 23, 104–5 of the Homer. If the class have a chance to read (or listen to) a translation of the complete boat-race episode (see 'Suggestions for further work' below), they may spot an indirect allusion to Homer at the start of the race, where Virgil illustrates the speed of the boats with an extended simile drawn from chariot-racing.

The gem shown on p. 144 is in the Museum of Fine Arts, Boston, U.S.A. The charioteer (in long dress) is turning the chariot. The Greek-vase fragment shown on p. 146 is in the National Museum, Athens. It depicts the funeral games in honour of Patroklos and his name and the name of the painter (Sophilos) can be picked out in the inscription (written in 'mirror writing'). The name of Achilles also appears on the right-hand edge. Pupils are usually intrigued to notice the four pairs of forelegs; if they look carefully they should also be able to distinguish the four heads. There is a more detailed description in Arias 285–6, illustration 39.

In addition to the illustrations in the pupil's text, further pictures of Greek chariot-racing (some of which refer specifically to the *Iliad* XXIII race) can be found in C.S.C.P. Greek Foundation Course Folder V (orange card 10 and green card 20), Harris plates 62–7, Swaddling 67, 69, 70 and Drees plates 4, 13a, 55 and V.

Suggestion for discussion

Why do you think Virgil used material from Homer? Why did he not simply make up his own story in his own words? (Coleman 119–20, Camps 9–10 and Woodman and West *passim*, especially 195–200, all have helpful remarks; it is worth stressing that Virgil's readers and listeners were usually intimately familiar with the Homeric poems, so that part of their pleasure in Virgil would come from recognising echoes of Homer and savouring Virgil's individual variations on Homeric themes and motifs.)

Vocabulary checklist

There are some opportunities here to revise linguistic points. From study of the nominative and genitive singular forms of *flūctus*, can the class deduce what declension it belongs to? What must the gender of *pondus* be, and what must be the form of its nominative and accusative plural? With *pondus–ponderōsus*, compare *pretium–pretiōsus*, *perīculum–perīculōsus*, *ōtium–ōtiōsus*, *aqua–aquōsus* and *spatium–spatiōsus*.

Suggestions for further work

1 The complete boat-race episode (*Aeneid* V.114–253) could be read in translation, including the presentation of prizes and the return of Sergestus, limping home in his crippled boat, as well as the elaborate similes (lines 144–7, 213–9) which were omitted from the pupil's text because of their linguistic complexity. If sufficient copies of the translation are available for pupils to refer to, they might study the similes in detail, deciding in each case what the points of resemblance are between the two things being compared.

2 The suggestion made on p. 66 above, that the class be asked to devise a 'shooting script' for filming the story they have just read, might be adopted here if not used already in connection with Daedalus and Icarus in Stage 44.

3 The class could invent another episode in the games, and write an account of it in prose or verse; it might be an event of their own choice or one specified by the teacher. As a variation on this, the teacher could first read a translation of the boxing-match in the Homeric games (*Iliad* XXIII.653–99), then ask the class to compose their own boxing-match narrative, and finally, for comparison with both Homer and the pupils' versions, read them Virgil's account (*Aeneid* V.362–484) of the fight between Dares and Entellus.

STAGE 48: NERŌ ET AGRIPPĪNA

Synopsis

Reading passages	Tacitus, *Annals* XIV.3–9 (adapted)
Background material	the emperor
Language notes	direct and indirect deliberative question historic infinitive perfect subjunctive passive

The reading material in this final Stage of the Course is taken from Tacitus' vivid and dramatic account of Nero's murder of Agrippina. Although the Latin has been adapted, it is hoped that sufficient flavour survives of the original to give pupils some impression of Tacitus' vigorous, colourful and quirky style. The selected passages offer much scope for considering such questions as 'Is it true? Should we believe this? Can we tell what really happened?' and for discussing the personality, behaviour and motives of the leading characters.

Title picture

Obverse of an *aureus* from the first year of Nero's reign, A.D. 54; Agrippina enjoys equal prominence with her son. The legend reads:
AGRIPP(INA) AVG(VSTA) DIVI CLAVD(II) NERONIS CAES(ARIS) MATER.

īnsidiae I (*Annals* XIV.3)

The commentaries of Woodcock and Furneaux will often be helpful during this Stage; Griffin (especially 23–49, 67–82), Warmington 43–8 and Woodcock 33–5 are very useful on the historical background.

The teacher may need to supplement the introduction in the pupil's text (p. 151) with some additional historical information, though care should be taken not to confuse the pupils by overdoing the detail. Nero was the son of Agrippina by Cn. Domitius Ahenobarbus, who died in A.D. 40. Agrippina's ambition was to secure her son's accession to the principate and become the power behind the throne. She married the Emperor Claudius, ensured the adoption of Nero into Claudius' family above the natural heir Britannicus (son of Claudius and Messalina) and arranged Nero's marriage to Claudius' daughter Octavia. When Claudius seemed to be contemplating the reinstatement of Britannicus as his heir, he died with suspicious suddenness; it was generally assumed that Agrippina was responsible. With the help of Burrus, she arranged for Britannicus to be kept in the background while Nero was hailed as emperor.

By A.D. 59, when the events described in Stage 48 took place, a three-cornered struggle for power had developed between Nero, his mother and the partnership of Burrus and Seneca (who for some time were effectively the rulers of the empire through their influence on Nero). One result of this struggle had been the poisoning of Britannicus, whom Agrippina had threatened to put in Nero's place. The situation was further complicated when Nero became infatuated with Poppaea. Both Nero and Poppaea were already married; Poppaea's husband Otho was removed from the scene by being sent to Spain as governor of Lusitania, but Nero's wife Octavia was a more serious obstacle to his plans. The marriage had originally been arranged by Agrippina, who was well aware that the divorce or murder of Octavia, followed by marriage between Nero and Poppaea, would be a clear sign that her own power and influence were on the wane. Burrus and Seneca watched the situation with concern, continuing to offer flattery, advice and support to Nero in order to check the power of Agrippina, while trying not to give too much power to Nero himself.

Relevant extracts from Tacitus, such as his accounts of the murders of Claudius (*Annals* XII.66–9) and Britannicus (XIII.15–16) might be read to the class in translation, for example in the versions of Grant (281–3, 290–1) or Tingay, *Empire* (68–9).

Notes

1 **vetustāte:** causal. Question 1 in the pupil's text might be expanded: 'Why was Nero confident enough to attempt the murder?'

Poppaeae: For details of her role in the crisis, see above.

3–4 **utrum ... ūterētur:** indirect deliberative question. A few examples have occurred earlier in the Course, and both direct and indirect deliberatives are discussed in the next language note. The captioned drawing may help the pupils, especially if the teacher asks 'What did Nero consult his advisers about?'

utrum ... an ... vel: Poison is contrasted with violence, which in turn is subdivided into (a) the sword (b) other violent methods. (For the combination *utrum ... an ... vel*, cf. Stage 41, p. 13, lines 3–4.)

6 **Britannicus:** see above.

7–8 **quō modō ... cēlārentur:** another indirect deliberative, this time preceding the main verb. Remind the pupils to read right through to *poterat* before attempting translation.

10 **Anicētus:** prefect of the fleet at Misenum.

11 **nāvem . . . compōnī:** Ask the class whether this is Tacitus' own comment or part of what Anicetus said (or elicit the same point by asking what is indicated by the fact that *nāvem* is accusative and *posse* infinitive).

11–12 **cuius pars . . . solūta . . . Agrippīnam ēiceret:** Comprehension questions may help: 'What was to happen to the ship? What would this do to Agrippina?'

13 **capāx fortuitōrum:** Note how pupils cope with the omission of *est*.

Question 2 in the pupil's text can be used to establish that Nero does not ask his advisers *whether* his mother should be killed; he asks them *how*. Tacitus' account of the consultations creates a lurid impression of the current state of the imperial court: poison is ruled out because Agrippina has anticipated it and fore-armed herself, and because after the killing of Britannicus any sudden death will arouse suspicion; the sword is ruled out because there is no one Nero can trust, either to do the killing or to keep it secret. Question 5 highlights the key features of Anicetus' scheme: it will make the murder look like an accident, and state religion will be used to conceal the author of the crime. The teacher might help pupils to appreciate the irony in Anicetus' speech by asking, 'In what tone of voice would you read *fortuitōrum* (line 13)? In a deadpan style? With a sneer? With heavy emphasis, as if the word were placed in inverted commas? Might any other words in Anicetus' speech be read in a similar tone?' (Possible answers could include *naufragiō*, line 13, and *pietātem*, line 16.)

Balme and Greenstock (90–5) have three passages and sets of comprehension questions on the murder of Agrippina. Their questions are a useful source of ideas for the teacher. (Sometimes rewording of the questions will be necessary, since Balme and Greenstock's adapted version of Tacitus differs in many details from the Stage 48 adaptation.)

The coin on p. 153 is an *aureus* of Nero and Agrippina, minted at Rome in A.D. 55, with the legend NERO CLAVD(II) DIVI F(ILIVS) CAES(AR) AVG(VSTVS) GERM(ANICVS) IMP(ERATOR) TR(IBVNICIA) P(OTESTATE) CO(N)S(VL). Agrippina, though still honoured by inclusion on the coin, is less dominant than in the coin on p. 149; she is placed behind Nero in the inferior position instead of facing him as before, and her titles are relegated to the reverse of the coin (whose legend is EX S(ENATVS) C(ONSVLTO) AGRIPP(INA) AVG(VSTA) DIVI CLAUD(II) NERONIS CAES(ARIS) MATER). Further portraits of Nero and Agrippina are shown on slides V.31–3.

Suggestions for consolidation: perfect passive participle in accusative (3; see also Appendix B); ablative of gerund (7, 16 (twice); further examples of gerund in ablative and genitive occur later in this Stage; see also Language Information, p. 214 of pupil's text); verb + nominative word order (4, 8, etc.; see also Appendix B); fear clause (3–9).

Vocabulary check: *at* (1); *fīō* (1); *cōnstituō* (2); *vel* (3, 16); *ūtor* (4); *inter* (4); *cāsus* (5); *cēlō* (8); *metuō* (8); *odiō est* (10); *ēiciō* (12); *adeō* (14).

īnsidiae II (*Annals* XIV.4)

Notes

2 **Bāiās:** for Baiae's reputation as a fashionable seaside resort, cf. the background material of Stage 45, p. 111 of pupil's text.
diem fēstum: The festival of the Quinquatrus was held in honour of Minerva from 19 to 23 March. It was celebrated by everybody whose employment was under the goddess' protection: schoolteachers and pupils, who had a school holiday; women and children in their role as spinners or weavers; artisans, artists, poets and painters.

3 **advenientī:** Position at front of sentence, and omission of *eī*, may cause trouble. An initial comprehension question such as 'What did Nero do?' may help.

4 **manū et complexū:** Establish the literal translation first, then encourage pupils to suggest more idiomatic versions, such as 'took her by the hand and embraced her', etc.

5 **stābat ... nāvis:** Attention to the emphatic word order here, especially if pupils are encouraged to reproduce it in translation ('Moored near the villa was a ship', etc.), will help bring out the point that this is 'the' ship, i.e. the booby-trapped one.

10–11 **iuxtā Nerōnem ... collocāta:** Pupils may be able to recall the way in which reclining diners were grouped at a formal Roman meal; cf. Paoli 92–3, Balsdon *Life* 35 and pupil's text Unit I, Stage 2, p. 12.

11–12 **modo ... modo:** If pupils are puzzled, they could be reminded of contexts where they met *modo ... modo* previously, e.g. the young Icarus who played *modo* with feathers, *modo* with wax (Stage 44, p. 74, lines 5–6), or the sparrow which hopped *modo hūc modo illūc* (Stage 45, p. 96, line 9). Reminders like this are often a valuable way of assisting pupils' recall of vocabulary and reinforcing their grasp of a word for future recollection.

13–14 **oculīs et pectorī haerēns:** It may be best to start with a literal version, then invite views on the question 'What does Tacitus *mean* by this phrase?' before settling on a final translation. Woodcock has 'hanging on her gaze and clinging to her breast'.

The logic of lines 1ff. may need to be made explicit to the class: by being on the coast Nero was already in the right place to put his plan into operation and the festival was a good excuse to persuade Agrippina to join him there.

The comings and goings in this chapter need to be carefully clarified for the pupils; relate the text where possible to the map. Tacitus' original narrative contains several obscurities and omissions (for example, he does not say where Nero met his mother before escorting her to Bauli), and in the interests of simplicity the version in the pupil's text has been heavily adapted; it also takes a liberty with Tacitus' account by making Agrippina arrive by land instead of sea. Nero meets his mother and escorts her to Bauli. The plan to bring her from Bauli to Baiae on the specially constructed ship is foiled, because she has got wind of Nero's intentions and decides to travel by land instead. However, when she leaves Baiae after the dinner and show of affection on Nero's part, the fatal ship has obviously been brought round to Baiae to await her, and she boards it for her return journey.

The map on p. 154 of the pupil's text could be related to the general map of the Bay of Naples area on p. 116. Slides V.35–8 show maps and views of Baiae and the Bay of Naples. The wall-painting reproduced on p. 155 of the pupil's text, from the house of M. Lucretius Fronto in Pompeii, is a stylised representation of the heavily-built-up coast. It shows many typical features of the wealthy people's residences along the Bay of Naples: jetties, harbours, colonnaded façades, towers, temples, statues, etc. Boats also feature frequently in such paintings, showing the important part that water transport played in everyday life.

Questions 2 and 5 can be used to draw pupils' attention to the skilful performance which Nero puts on to win his mother over. He goes to meet her and embraces her, but this is not enough; the rumour of treachery arouses her suspicions, and she chooses a safer method of travel to Baiae. Nero eventually succeeds in reassuring her with his blandishments, sometimes putting on an act of affectionate playfulness (*familiāritāte iuvenīlī*, line 11) and sometimes pretending to treat her as a respected adviser by discussing serious matters (*graviter loquēbātur*, line 12). Discussion of question 6 should help to make it clear that Nero is either rounding off his performance with a hypocritical final embrace or genuinely moved at the sight of his mother going to her death (though if the second explanation is true Tacitus still adds a last jibe with *saevum* in line 15 – *ferum* in the original text).

Suggestions for consolidation: gerundive (2, 3, 6, 14; see also Language Information, pp. 214–15 of pupil's text); 3rd person perfect in *-ēre* (10); verb + nominative word order (1, 6; see also Appendix B); locative (7; the examples in Language Information, p. 206 of pupil's text, might be tackled at this point of not studied already).

Vocabulary check: *occāsiō* (1); *obviam eō* (4); *excipiō* (4, 10); *quasi* (5); *cēlō* (7); *vehō* (9); *metus* (10); *iuxtā* (10); *collocō* (11); *mē gerō* (11); *abeō* (13); *vel . . . vel* (14); *animus* (15).

First language note (direct and indirect deliberative question)

The captioned illustration on p. 152 of the pupil's text may provide a convenient starting-point for discussion of this feature.

Further examples:

direct

1 *utrum pugnēmus an fugiāmus?*
2 *quōs deōs precēmur?*
3 *quō modō inimīcōs meōs fallam?*

indirect

1 *senex nesciēbat quot hospitēs ad cēnam invītāret.*
2 *incertus sum quantum praemium servīs dem.*
3 *iuvenēs mercātōrem rogāvērunt unde pecūniam adipīscerentur.*

Some pupils may ask 'How can I tell an indirect question from an indirect deliberative, since they both have verbs in the subjunctive?' The best answer may be to get them to study and discuss a particular example, such as sentence 3 in paragraph 2: which is the likelier meaning, 'unsure whether to give way' or 'unsure whether they were giving way'? Examples like these illustrate the point that ambiguity is normally prevented by the context. (If the context does not make the meaning plain, ambiguity can be avoided by phrasing the sentence differently, e.g. by using the gerundive of obligation instead of a deliberative.)

naufragium I (*Annals* XIV.5–6)

Notes

2 **nāvis:** not described by Tacitus; probably an open boat with a canopy or shelter towards the stern for Agrippina and her companions.

4 **gubernāculō:** probably easiest taken as dative after *adstābat*. If pupils are unsure how it fits into the clause, ask 'Where was Crepereius standing?'

5 **cubitantis recumbēns:** Use comprehension questions to establish that these participles refer to Agrippina and Acerronia respectively. Acerronia was sitting on or beside the foot of the couch and leaning across Agrippina's feet.

6 **cum datō signō . . .:** After the long parenthesis *duōbus . . . commemorābat* (lines 3–6), the class may need to be reminded of the sentence's opening words *nec multum erat prōgressa nāvis*, line 2.

ruere tēctum . . . grave: The weighted canopy is intended to crush the couch's occupants and/or knock a hole in the bottom of the boat (with the help, if necessary, of those sailors who are in the plot) so that Agrippina is shot into the water as originally planned. Pupils could be invited to illustrate their own ideas about the murder mechanism on the blackboard; they should be encouraged throughout this passage to visualise the scene.

8 **prōtēctae sunt:** They were both lower than the sides of the couch, which were too strongly built to give way beneath the weight of the collapsing canopy.

9 **turbātīs omnibus:** causal. Tacitus typically varies the construction by continuing with a *quod*-clause; the question 'Why did the ship not break up?' may help.

11–12 **eīs . . . cōnsēnsus:** Accept such renderings as 'there was no agreement among them', etc.; the use of the possessive dative might be discussed and analysed later.

14 **dum . . . clāmat:** Either ask the class 'What did Acerronia shout?' or read the whole clause through to *clāmat* and ask for a translation.

16 **minus agnita:** By keeping quiet, she ensured that as few people as possible would notice or recognise her (but the fact that she was wounded suggests that she did not go completely unrecognised).

18 **vīllam:** probably Bauli.

19ff. **animadverterat enim ...:** Note how pupils cope with the numerous examples of indirect statement in this paragraph.

20–1 **summā suī parte:** The 'accident' originated well above deck. Agrippina realised that if it had been a genuine accident, caused by the sea (e.g. if the sea had carried the ship onto a rock), the damage would have been more likely to originate below deck, in the ship's hull.

21 **velut terrestre māchināmentum:** A building or contraption on land might suffer damage to its upper part and collapse downwards (unlike a ship – see previous note). But Tacitus could also be referring to stage machinery (in keeping with Nero's theatrical interests) or to the device constructed in some private houses which allowed ceilings to open and shower presents over amazed guests.

23 **sī ... vidērētur:** defines *remēdium*.

25 **fortūnā eius:** *eius* refers to Nero. The emperor was felt to embody the luck of the Roman people; an individual's good fortune was bound up with, and dependent on, the emperor's *fortūna*. It was therefore plausible for Agrippina to say, albeit with heavy irony, that she had escaped disaster thanks to providence and Nero's good luck. She also implied, equally ironically, that her survival was a piece of good fortune *for* Nero.

26–7 **sibi ... quiēte opus esse:** Establish that the indirect statement is still continuing. Pupils may need reminding of the meaning of *opus est*; a simpler example (e.g. *opus est mihi pecūniā*) may help.

28 **testāmentum ... requīrātur:** evidently expecting that there was something in Acerronia's will for her. (Tacitus, *Annals* XII.7 refers to Agrippina's *cupido auri immensa*.)

Use question 1 to establish the logic of Tacitus' first sentence: the night was bright and clear and the sea was calm, so the sudden disintegration of a ship would automatically arouse suspicion.

The second part of question 2 may help pupils to appreciate the ironical way in which Acerronia's joy at the feigned repentance of Nero is juxtaposed with the collapse of the roof. Tacitus builds up the picture slowly and in detail, then abruptly shatters the calm scene with violent action; the class might be asked to compare the number of words devoted to scene-setting with the number of words describing the catastrophe. Acerronia's action (referred to in question 4) could be interpreted as a counter-productive attempt at self-preservation or as a heroic self-sacrifice, designed to distract Agrippina's enemies from their intended victim (an interpretation consistent with the facts as reported by Tacitus, though not with his authorial comment *imprūdenter*, line 14).

Question 5 involves the extraction of a lot of material from lines 19–22; it may be convenient to list the relevant points on the blackboard. Question 6 seeks to bring out the fact that Agrippina is trying as hard as she can to convince Nero that she has not realised that the 'shipwreck' was a murder attempt (cf. *sī nōn intellegere vidērētur*, line 23).

After tackling question 7, the class might consider whether it is appalling or admirable that someone who has just avoided death by a hair's breadth, who has had to swim for her life and who has realised that her own son has tried to kill her and may well try again, can still take time to investigate whether her murdered friend has left her a legacy. This could lead to question 8 and discussion of Agrippina's character. *silēns* (line 16) neatly distinguishes her from the chaos around her; her quick appreciation of the situation and the bold resourcefulness of her escape from the ship contrast pointedly with her assailants' messy bungling. On reaching temporary safety, she thinks fast and effectively, formulating her plan and putting it into operation by sending her message to Nero, describing him (perhaps with a certain grim relish at the irony) as *perīculō mātris perterritus*. The deceptions which Nero had practised to lure his mother to her death (his pretended reconciliation and friendliness at the dinner, followed by the fake 'shipwreck'), are matched by equally shrewd and barefaced deceitfulness on her part (cf. in particular *vidērētur*, line 23, and *simulātiōnem*, line 29). The mother takes her son on at his own game.

Encourage translations that reproduce the final epigrammatic brevity of *hoc sōlum nōn per simulātiōnem* (lines 28–9), e.g. '– her only sincere action'.

For further possible questions, see Balme and Greenstock 92–3.

Suggestions for consolidation: 3rd person plural perfect in *-ēre* (1, 12; cf. 'īnsidiae' II, p. 154, line 10, and see examples in Language Information, p. 189 of pupil's text); deliberative question (19); possessive dative (11; see also Language Information, p. 205 of pupil's text and p. 128 below); verb of speaking following indirect statement (14; see also Language Information, pp. 209–10 of pupil's text and p. 129 below); several examples of indirect statement (19–27; see also Language Information, pp. 209–11 of pupil's text); *quī* introducing purpose clause (24).

Vocabulary check: *sīdus* (1); *praebeō* (1); *quasi* (2); *patefaciō* (2); *comitor* (3); *haud* (4, 17); *procul* (4, 17); *plērīque* (9); *latus* (11); *agnōscō* (16); *excipiō* (17); *quīdam* (17); *vehō* (18); *animadvertō* (19); *lītus* (20); *velut* (21); *ēvādō* (25); *cāsus* (25); *opus est* (27); *requīrō* (28).

naufragium II (*Annals* XIV.7)

Notes

1 **Nerōnī . . . exspectantī:** a difficult example of dative noun and present participle at the front of the sentence. Ask 'What was Nero doing? What happened while he was waiting? What news was brought?'

5–6 **num . . . iubērentur:** Note how pupils cope with the indirect deliberative.

6 **praetōriānōs:** Pupils may need reminding that they were, among other things, the emperor's bodyguard (see picture on p. 160).

7 **obstrictōs esse:** For the military oath, sworn by the recruit on enlistment and renewed (in abbreviated form) on 1 January each year, see Watson 49–50; the class may recall it from Stage 41, p. 12, line 4. Burrus evidently felt (or pretended to feel) that the praetorian guard's oath of loyalty extended beyond the emperor to members of the imperial family.

8 **Germānicī:** much loved by the soldiery and, according to Tacitus (*Annals* II.82–3), widely mourned on his premature death. Slide V.32 shows a cameo of Agrippina's family, including Germanicus.

10 **illō diē:** emphatic. Nero's original word (in *oratio recta*) was *hodiē* – 'Today I become emperor at last.'
darī: present passive infinitive with past (historic present) verb of speaking; if it causes trouble, a simplified version may help, e.g. *Nerō dīxit imperium sibi darī.*
imperium: supreme power, the emperorship.

The questions in the pupil's text are not intended as comprehension questions for use on initial reading; they presuppose that the passage has already been read and translated. Discussion will probably centre on the behaviour of the characters. Nero's consultation with his advisers reads like a parody of the *cōnsilium prīncipis*, in which Tacitus pursues two favourite themes: the corruption of the imperial court, and Nero's unfitness to govern. Whereas Agrippina was shown in the previous passage thinking and acting with great calm and decisiveness, Nero immediately panics on learning of her escape. Equally revealing is the reaction of Burrus and Seneca – *longum utrīusque silentium* (line 4). It would be highly dangerous for them to try to dissuade Nero from going ahead with the murder, and equally dangerous to be his accomplices in so extreme a crime. Furthermore, if Agrippina is to be killed forthwith, the problem remains: who is to do the deed? Not the army, for reasons given by Burrus in lines 6–8. With what sounds like a sudden inspiration in the last three words of his speech, Burrus thrusts the responsibility onto Anicetus, who is more than ready to arrange the murder of his old enemy (cf. 'īnsidiae' I, p. 153, line 10).

Pupils will probably notice how the volatile Nero switches at once from panic to euphoria. In lines 2–3 he was hysterical with terror; by lines 11–12 he is giving orders. Also noticeable is the emphatic word order in lines 10–11, culminating in *lībertum* – power at Rome is now the gift of a freedman.

The question of Tacitus' reliability could also be raised. How could he possibly have known what Nero and his advisers said? Most or all of them were dead long before Tacitus wrote. Does this mean that he made the episode up? If so, is his history worthless?

The photograph on p. 160 shows members of the praetorian guard, from a 1st-century relief in the Louvre. The guards are depicted in their distinctive dress uniform, worn for ceremonial occasions and, like that of the British royal Guards today, old-fashioned compared with what they wore on operational service. Note particularly the comparative lack of body armour, the decorated helmets with large plumes and the oval shields decorated in the Republican manner (operational shields were rectangular by this date). The man second from left is wearing a large medal (*phalera*) which was a decoration for bravery. Behind the men can be seen their eagle standard. The praetorian guard were paid more than three times as much as regular legionaries and also received peace-time bonuses, e.g. when a new emperor came to power. They were considered an elite and were definitely a power to be reckoned with in the city (see also background material in the pupil's text, pp. 170–1).

Suggestions for consolidation: dative noun and participle at start of sentence (1; cf. 'īnsidiae' II, p. 154, line 3; two more examples will be met in the next passage); omission of *erat* (4; cf. 'naufragium' I, p. 158, lines 28–9; a further example will be met in the next passage); verb of speaking placed after indirect statement (7; cf. 'naufragium' I, p. 158, line 14 and see also Language Information, pp. 210–11 of pupil's text and p. 129 below); jussive subjunctive (8; see Language Information, p. 208 of pupil's text and p. 129 below).

Vocabulary check: *pavor* (2); *ultiō* (3); *uterque* (4); *respiciō* (5); *adversus* (7); *efficiō* (8); *haudquāquam* (9); *poscō* (9); *imperium* (10); *auctor* (10); *mūnus* (11); *proficīscor* (12).

Second language note (historic infinitive)

It is worth making the point that historic infinitives are normally used in pairs or groups (either within the same sentence or in successive sentences) rather than singly. The sentence from Sallust quoted in paragraph 2 is translated by Woodcock (*New Latin Syntax* 15) as '... a dreadful scene in the open plains: pursuit – flight – (men) being slaughtered and taken prisoner', which reflects very clearly the terseness and rapidity that can be achieved by such a series of infinitives.

Several examples of the historic infinitive occur in the next reading passage.

percussōrēs (*Annals* XIV.8–9)

Quinn (*Latin Explorations* 115–27) has a very helpful and detailed discussion of this passage. Balme and Warman 59–60, and Balme and Greenstock 94–5, contain numerous ideas for questions.

Notes

2 **hī mōlēs ... cōnscendere:** If the need to supply *cōnscendere* with *mōlēs* as well as *scaphās* causes trouble, the teacher might quote a simpler example, e.g. *aliī cibum, aliī vīnum laudāvērunt.*
mōlēs: 'the long dike that separated the Lucrine lake from the sea' (Woodcock).

5 **dīversa ... incerta:** Use comprehension questions to encourage such translations as 'asking various things, asking various questions' and 'replying uncertainly, making uncertain answers'.

15 **triērarchō ... centuriōne:** the former commanded the ship, the latter (*centuriō classiārius* in full) the marines.

21 **convīvālī lectō:** Normally a special couch (*lectus fūnebris*) would be used.

25 **astrologī:** Originally from Assyria, they established themselves in large towns throughout the empire, wherever human gullibility and superstition could earn them a living. Officially banned, they were occasionally expelled (but never for long, as Tacitus points out, *Histories* I.22). Cf. Unit IIB Handbook, p. 68, and Unit IIIB pupil's text, p. 81, Handbook, p. 134.

Some suggested questions

What is the mood of the crowd on the sea-shore? How does it change? Is it easy to visualise the scene?

Who are the *hominēs armātī et minantēs* (line 8)? (With a little help, pupils should be able to identify them with the *hominēs fidēlissimī* mentioned by Nero in 'naufragium' II, p. 159, line 12.)

How many words in lines 8–11 indicate violent action?

How often does the scene change in lines 1–20? (Pupils might in particular note the narrative sequence in lines 9–17, reminiscent of a familiar cinema technique. We follow the assassins to the victim's door; then go back slightly in time to accompany the victim through the moments before the assassins' arrival (and, unlike the victim, we know how imminent the end is). Finally, the two sequences of events come together for the climax: 'The maid makes to go away; Agrippina's gaze follows her to the door – and falls on Anicetus standing there with his thugs . . . The assassins say nothing.' (Quinn *LE* 124))

Why does Tacitus mention that the room was dimly lit (lines 11–12)?

What is the significance of Agrippina's last words and action? Does she wish to avoid disfigurement in death (cf. Quinn *LE* 119) or is it a symbolic gesture?

Why was Agrippina given such a hasty funeral? (Pupils might consider the danger to Nero from a popular outcry provoked by a full-scale public funeral or a hostile and emotional funeral oration.)

What rumour does Tacitus report? (His use of innuendo in lines 21–3 is very characteristic: he refrains from positive assertion but takes care that the reader is informed of the discreditable story.)

At what point (if any) do the class feel sympathy for Agrippina? If sympathy is evoked by her vulnerability in lines 13–14 and the account of her murder in lines 17–20, is it dispelled by the final anecdote in lines 23–7? What does the anecdote suggest about Agrippina's character? Is it consistent with the impression of her character created during the Stage as a whole?

The coin reproduced on p. 163 of the pupil's text is an *aureus* of Nero, minted at Rome A.D. 64–8. The obverse shows the head of Nero, wearing a laurel wreath; the reverse (not included in the pupil's text) shows a seated figure of the goddess Salus. The coin may commemorate Nero's deliverance from the great fire of Rome in A.D. 64 or his escape from the conspiracy of Piso in A.D. 65. Similar coins might have been issued at the time of Agrippina's murder as part of the general thanksgiving (described in *Annals* XIV.12–13) for Nero's alleged 'narrow escape'. Pupils might compare this one with those illustrated on pp. 149 and 153, commenting on the differences between the three coins.

Suggestions for consolidation: historic infinitive (pupils might be asked to pick out the seven historic infinitives in lines 1–8, referring back to the language note on p. 161 of their text if necessary and noting how the infinitive is used to unfold a scene of hurried activity); dative pronoun and participle at start of sentence (18, 24; cf. 'naufragium' II, p. 159, line 1); jussive subjunctive (26); verb + nominative word order (5–6; see also Appendix B); substantival participle (11; see Language Information, p. 211 of pupil's text and p. 130 below); verb of speaking, etc. following indirect statement or question (7, 23, 24 (the effect of the second example might be analysed: Tacitus gives the rumour in detail before casting any doubt on it); see also Language Information, p. 210 of pupil's text and p. 129 below).

Vocabulary check: *interim* (1); *nōnnūllī* (3); *compleō* (4); *dīversus* (5); *lūmen* (6, 12); *incolumis* (6); *dōnec* (7, 10); *magis ac magis* (12); *abeō* (13); *comitor* (15); *īdem* (21); *vīlis* (21); *ut* + indicative (22).

Third language note (perfect subjunctive passive)

The caption to the illustration on p. 162 of the pupil's text may provide a convenient starting-point for discussion; other examples of the perfect subjunctive passive met by the pupils are *lēctī sint* (Stage 41, p. 13, lines 3–4) and the deponent *admīrātus sit* (Stage 48, p. 163, line 23). Invite comment on the way the tense is formed. For further practice, pupils could convert indicative examples such as *necātī sunt*, *prohibita est* and *secūtī sumus* into the corresponding subjunctive forms, and work out the subjunctive forms of 'you (s.) have been called', 'I have been sent', 'they (fem.) have used', etc. with the aid of the information given under *vocō*, *mittō*, *ūtor*, etc. in Part III of the Language Information section.

Manipulation exercises

Exercise 1 Type: translation from English, using restricted pool of Latin words

Linguistic features being practised: dative of present participle, *īdem*, vocative, gerund, comparative adverb, *nisi*, conditional sentences with indicative, 2nd person plural future passive, jussive subjunctive, present infinitive of deponent verb, genitive of *hic*, *fīō*

Encourage pupils to refer to the Language Information section in cases of doubt.

Exercise 2 Type: transformation

Linguistic features being practised: present, imperfect, pluperfect and perfect subjunctive passive, introduced in Stages 41, 43, 46 and 48; nominative and ablative cases

It may be useful to discuss the reason why *ā* (*ab*) is used in sentences 1b, 4b, 5b and 6b but not in 2b and 3b; ask pupils what *servī*, *hostēs*, *barbarī* and *prīnceps*, but not *flammae* and *inopia*, have in common. They might also be asked to explain why a subjunctive is used in each example, referring if necessary to the Language Information section, pp. 207–8.

If the teacher opts to give this exercise to the class before they have read the final reading passage, 'percussōrēs', and the last language note, they will probably need help with sentence 6b. It requires the formation of a perfect subjunctive passive, which appears only at the very end of the reading material.

The background material

Garnsey and Saller 1–6, 15–20, 35–9 give a very useful brief guide. Millar's vast work (if the teacher has access to a copy) will provide a rich store of illustrative material, thoroughly analysed; see in particular 59–131 (the emperor's assistants), 203–72 (the emperor at work) and 465–549 (the emperor's dealings with private individuals). Millar demonstrates that communication between an emperor and his subjects was normally initiated by the latter; they approached the emperor with their petitions or disputes, and he responded.

The teacher might write up the names (and perhaps dates) of some 1st- and early 2nd-century emperors on the blackboard, and prompt the class to recall details or incidents in connection with each emperor, either from earlier Stages in the Course, or from elsewhere. For example:

Augustus: huge building programme (mentioned in Stage 30); patron of Virgil (Stage 36); marriage laws (38); banishes Ovid (39).

Claudius: launches invasion of Britain (14); rebukes Alexandrian rioters (17); his temple at Colchester destroyed by Iceni (23); extensive use of freedmen (34); murdered by Agrippina (48).

Nero: initiates inquiry into riot at Pompeii, dismisses Pompeian *duovirī* and appoints a *praefectus* (8, 11); persecutes Christians (33); murders mother (48).

Vespasian: perhaps rewards Cogidubnus with palace for loyalty (15); building programme, including start of Colosseum (30); punishes Helvidius Priscus (35).

Titus: Pompeii destroyed during his reign (12); sacks Jerusalem (29).

Domitian: sends Salvius to Britain (13); dedicates Arch of Titus (29); has Paris killed and Domitia exiled (34); triumphs over Germans, punishes Vestal Virgins (35); flattered by Martial (36); recalls Agricola (37); adopts Clemens' sons (38); kills flies (39).

Trajan: policy on Christians (33); correspondence with Pliny (41).

The teacher may like to start with open-ended questions such as 'What can you remember about Claudius?', then prompt the pupils' memories with more specific questions such as 'In whose reign was Pompeii destroyed? Which poet did Augustus send into exile?' etc.

Our sources' numerous anecdotes about emperor–subject relationships are often vivid and illuminating; many could be tracked down by pupils (under guidance) from translations of Tacitus, Suetonius and Pliny. They might include Suetonius, *Augustus* 53 (Augustus teases a timid petitioner); Philo, *Legatio ad Gaium* 44–5 (the Jewish embassy from Alexandria traipses frustratedly round the imperial gardens after Caligula); Suetonius, *Claudius* 18 (Claudius pelted with stale crusts by a mob in the forum during a corn shortage); Tacitus, *Annals* XIII.5 (Agrippina's attempt to sit next to Nero when he receives the Armenian envoys); Tacitus, *Annals* XIV.17 (Nero's response to the riot in Pompeii); Suetonius, *Vespasian* 23 (Vespasian's mule-driver is bribed by a man who wants to petition the emperor; Vespasian demands a half-share of the bribe); Pliny, *Letters* X.2–13 (miscellaneous requests to Trajan, made by Pliny on behalf of himself or others); Historia Augusta, *Hadrian* 17, quoted by Balsdon, *Life* 30 (Hadrian treats an ex-soldier kindly during a casual visit to the baths, but refuses to repeat his generosity on a wider scale). The extraordinary range of the requests made to the emperor is well illustrated by the petition of the Balearic islanders (Pliny the Elder, *Natural History* VIII. 81.218) asking Augustus for military assistance against a plague of rabbits.

The bridge at Alcantara shown on p. 168 is generally thought the finest example in the Roman world. It crosses the river Tagus and was built about A.D. 106, entirely without mortar. The bridge is about 200 metres (655 ft) long and the spans rise nearly 50 metres (165 ft) above the river.

The succession. Pupils may recall Domitian's adoption of Clemens' sons from Stage 38. It is not known whether they predeceased Domitian or were ignored or murdered after his assassination. Nerva's adoption of Trajan (pupil's text, p. 172) was a response to pressure by the army and perhaps a (successful) attempt to forestall a military coup.

Emperor-worship. Lewis and Reinhold II.560–8 have a useful collection of source material. See in particular Herodian's description of an emperor's apotheosis (ibid. 565–6), culminating in the release from the blazing pyre of an eagle symbolising the emperor's soul (cf. Unit IIA, p. 50 of pupil's text).

The class could study the coins illustrated on pp. 149, 153 and 163 of their text, and discuss the explanations for some of the emperor's titles, such as *Caesar*, *Augustus* and *imperātor*, and the reason why emperors took *tribūnicia potestās*. Emperors' use of the coinage for propaganda purposes could also be considered, and illustrated either from earlier Units or from any other convenient source. Coins made it possible to familiarise the inhabitants of Italy and the provinces with the emperor's physical features, titles, achievements (e.g. the conquest of Britain, Unit IIIA, p. 49; the defeat of the Jews, Unit IIIB, p. 9; and the building of the *via Trāiāna*, slide IV.39) and political slogans (e.g. from the civil war of A.D. 69, *pax orbis terrarum* on a denarius of Otho and *Roma resurgens* on a sestertius of Vespasian, both shown in Royal Academy exhibition catalogue nos. 1(n) and 1(p); further examples on front cover and first page of Jones).

Encourage the pupils to interpret the details of the picture on p. 171 of their text. In the centre, between Marcus Aurelius and the piper (whose function is to drown inauspicious noises during the sacrifice) is the *camillus*, a young man of noble family chosen to assist in the ritual; he carries an open box of incense. The man with the axe is the *popa*, who will kill the ox; his colleague holds up a vessel in which the victim's heart, lungs and liver will be cooked, after inspection by the *haruspicēs*. For further details, see C.S.C.P. *The Roman World*, Teacher's Handbook 2, 51; see also Unit IIIA, p. 55 of pupil's text.

The cameo gem illustrated on p. 173 is also full of detail. It is 25 cm (10 inches) wide. The top row shows Augustus and Roma enthroned side by side, his birth sign of Capricorn between them. The group of three figures behind him is usually interpreted as Oikoumene, the civilised world, placing a wreath on his head, bearded Ocean, and Earth with horn of plenty and a child on either side. Under the throne is the Eagle, bird of Jupiter. On the left, Tiberius in toga and holding a sceptre steps out of a chariot (this may refer to his victory over the Germans and Pannonians in A.D. 12). Behind him is Victory, with outspread wings. The young man in armour next to Roma may be Germanicus. In the lower row four soldiers erect a trophy with a captive man and woman seated on the left, while on the right two soldiers seize another couple by their hair. The cameo must have been made either after Augustus' death or for the provinces, as Augustus did not permit in Rome the cult of himself as Jupiter with the goddess Roma.

Suggestions for discussion

1 What are the advantages and disadvantages of giving supreme power to one man? (Cf. Tacitus' description of the principate and personal freedom as *res olim dissociabiles* in *Agricola* 3.)

2 Why did emperors put up with such a heavy work-load instead of simply delegating the decision-making to other people? (Encourage a

variety of answers: it might be suggested, for instance, that if emperors delegated their work they would be delegating (and diminishing) their power; or that they enjoyed being regarded as powerful and paternalistic rulers, personally concerned for their subjects' welfare; or that they were impelled by a sense of duty. Tiberius might be quoted as an example of an emperor who did delegate the running of the empire to others when he retired to Capri; the subsequent conspiracy (real or alleged) of Sejanus illustrates the danger of such delegation.)

3 Compare the different methods of choosing an emperor, described on p. 172. Which way seems to you most likely to produce a good emperor? Is there anything to be said in favour of the other methods?

Vocabulary checklist

Pupils might revise *sī quis/quid* as well as *nē quis/quid*, and the teacher could reinforce *velut* by reminding them of examples met in their reading; for example, Daedalus flew ahead of Icarus *velut āles* (Stage 44, p. 78, line 4) and Catullus' love died *velut . . . flōs* (Stage 45, p. 105, lines 22–3). With *metuere–metus* compare *redīre–reditus*, *advenīre–adventus*, *currere–cursus*, *rīdēre–rīsus*, etc. Numbers can be practised by a 'mental arithmetic' game, in which each pupil is allocated one of the numerals on page 174; the teacher then calls out a pair of numbers (e.g. *novem* and *quīnque*) to be added together, and the pupil to whom the required numeral has been allocated (in this case *quattuordecim*) identifies himself or herself by raising a hand, standing up or calling out the number. As a variation, the class can be required to subtract one number from another, or to multiply (using *bis* and *ter*).

Suggestions for further work

1 The whole Nero and Agrippina episode from *Annals* XIV might be read in translation; this could be followed by a discussion of Tacitus' reliability. Able pupils would enjoy Paterson's sceptical discussion in *Omnibus* 6, pp. 23–5.

2 The class could consider the problem: 'If Nero was really so unsatisfactory, why was it difficult to get rid of him?' The question raises several issues: absolute power and the means by which that power was supported, notably the army and the Praetorian Guard; respect for the office, if not for the man; the difficulty of agreeing about a successor, caused partly by the removal, at the beginning of his reign, of any obvious rivals.

3 Ask the class to compose appeals or petitions to the emperor; their aim should be to make it as difficult as possible for him to say no. Each

request could be an amplification of one of the examples given on pp. 169–70 of their text, or could be based on some other situation suggested by the teacher or invented by the pupils themselves. (Some pupils may like to work in pairs, each member of the pair presenting one side of a dispute.) Some of the appeals and petitions might be read out to the class, for pupils to assess their persuasiveness.

4 Pupils might look at newspaper reports and articles about speeches and activities of politicians or members of the royal family who happen to be in the news at the time, noting the various reporting styles (serious, chatty, scurrilous, propagandist, etc.) and comparing them with our sources' diverse treatment of the emperors (including official pronouncements by the emperors themselves, for which see, e.g., Lewis and Reinhold II.119 and 130–1).

The Language Information section

As in previous Units, this Section has two functions:

(a) reference by the pupils, e.g. while doing manipulation exercises or preparing a reading passage;
(b) consolidation during the later stages of Unit IVB.

It includes comment on five linguistic features that have occurred in the material without being discussed in the Stage language notes: the possessive dative; the locative case; indirect statement without an introductory verb of speaking; conditional sentences with present and imperfect subjunctive; subordinate clauses in indirect statement. Each of these features could be studied, at a point convenient to the teacher, during the reading of the later Stages of the Unit.

Examples of various linguistic features which have been discussed in the text but often need further practice, have been collected from the text of Unit IVB and placed in this section of the Handbook under the relevant sub-heading; they may be useful either for 'first aid' or for consolidation. It is usually advisable for the teacher, when using these examples, to refer pupils primarily to those sentences which they have already met in their reading (on the principle of using the familiar to elucidate the unfamiliar); but sometimes, provided that the teacher supplies some context, the pupils might, for extra practice, try their hand at examples drawn from Stages which they have not yet read. Appendix B collects some further examples of linguistic features (mainly variations of word order) that do not appear in the Language Information section.

Accidence

Nouns (pp. 178–9). Pupils might revise these by translating some simple sentences into Latin ('the king's slaves showed the city to the merchant', etc.), working either on their own or in pairs or together as a class. Sentences should initially be restricted to the nouns in the paradigms and two or three verbs such as *dedit/dedērunt*, *ostendit/ostendērunt*; further words can be progressively added by the teacher to suit the pupils' proficiency.

Pronouns (pp. 184–7). Examples of *is quī* (paragraph 9) from Unit IVB text:

... *eīs operibus quae* ... Stage 41, p. 5, line 7.
... *id quod prius accidit* ... St. 41, p. 10, line 12.

... *culpa est penes eōs quī* ... St. 41, p. 13, lines 5–6.
... *nōmen dederimus eīs quī* ... St. 41, p. 18, line 4.
... *ea quae* ... *auxiliō esse possint.* St. 41, p. 18, line 6
(compare *ille* ... *vidētur, quī* ... in Stage 45, p. 92, lines 1–3).
... *scelerī id assignet quod* ... St. 48, p. 153, lines 14–15.
... *eōs impediēbant quī* ... St. 48, p. 157, line 10.
... *eōs abripit quī obstant.* St. 48, p. 162, lines 9–10.

Examples where antecedent is deferred or omitted:

quās ... *mōverat aura, captābat plūmās.* St. 44, p. 74, lines 5–6.
quī ... *possent, crēdidit esse deōs.* St. 44, p. 78, lines 10–11.
quod vidēs perīsse perditum dūcās. St. 45, p. 102, line 2.
nec quae fugit sectāre ... St. 45, p. 102, line 10.

Verbs (pp. 188–99). For suggestions on helping pupils with the terminology ('indicative', 'passive', etc.), see Unit IVA Handbook p. 51. The aim is not to provide definitions (which are normally too abstract to be much help) but to enable pupils to find their way around these pages.

Syntax

Uses of the cases (pp. 204–6). Paragraphs 3c and 6e can be used to revise the syntax of *in*. It could be pointed out that *super* and *sub*, like *in*, are used with either the accusative or the ablative, depending on their meaning; ask the class what case 'table' would be, if 'the cat was asleep under the table' were turned into Latin, or what case 'moon' would be, in 'the cow jumped over the moon'.

Examples of the possessive dative (paragraph 5e):

... *mihi erat tanta cupiditās aut necessitās* ... ? St. 43, p. 60, line 13.
... *est mihi memoria tuī.* St. 43, p. 61, line 6.
nōbīs ... *nūllum cōnsilium abeundī erat* ... St. 46, p. 120, lines 21–2.
dī, quibus imperium est pelagī ... St. 47, p. 138, line 11.
nōn ... *eīs erat prōmptus* ... *cōnsēnsus.* St. 48, p. 157, lines 11–12.

Examples of the ablative of comparison (paragraph 6f):

rīsū St. 42, p. 32, line 14.
oculīs St. 45, p. 96, line 5.
saxō ... *undā* St. 42, p. 40, line 7.
Notō ... *sagittā* St. 47, p. 138, line 18.

Examples of the locative case (paragraph 7):

Pergamī St. 41, p. 3, line 3.
Nīcomēdiae St. 41, p. 16, line 2.
Bāiīs St. 48, p. 154, line 7.
Rōmae St. 41, p. 5, line 8.
Ephesī St. 43, p. 53, line 1.

With the help of the explanation of the locative's formation in paragraph 7, the class might work out the Latin for 'at Chester', 'at Alexandria', 'at Herculaneum', 'at Athens', 'at Carthage', etc., with the teacher supplying nominative and genitive forms where needed.

Uses of the subjunctive (pp. 207–8). Examples of indirect question preceding the verb of asking, etc. (paragraph 2):

mātrōnae quid accidisset exposuit. St. 43, p. 55, lines 6–7.
quārē id faciam, fortasse requīris. St. 45, p. 101, line 1.
num īnspexerit . . . et . . . admīrātus sit, incertum est. St. 48, p. 163, lines 21–3.

Examples of the jussive subjunctive (paragraph 8):

vīvāmus . . . amēmus . . . aestimēmus. St. 45, p. 93, lines 1–3.
dēsinās . . . dūcās. St. 45, p. 102, lines 1–2.
vīvat valeatque . . . nec . . . respectet . . . St. 45, p. 105, lines 17–21.
'*dēflectāmus . . .*' St. 46, p. 120, line 3.
'*efficiat Anicētus . . .*' St. 48, p. 159, line 8.
'*occīdat . . . dum imperet.*' St. 48, p. 163, lines 26–7.

For further examples of the jussive subjunctive, see p. 71 above.

Note how the class cope with the various examples of passive and deponent forms included in paragraph 9, and make up further examples if necessary.

Indirect statement (pp. 209–11). If pupils enquire about the future infinitive passive, confirm that it exists but is seldom met. They might be asked to explain in their own words why *sē* is used in sentences 1 and 2 of paragraph 3 but *eum* in sentences 5 and 6; and they might use sentences 7 and 8 to practise the two ways of translating *negō* given in paragraph 2.

Examples where the verb of speaking, etc. is placed after or in the middle of the indirect statement:

mātrōnam esse pulcherrimam . . . animadverterat. St. 43, p. 54, line 28.
nūllī sē dīcit mulier mea nūbere mālle . . . St. 45, p. 98, line 1.
mare . . . resorbērī vidēbāmus. St. 46, p. 116, line 3.
. . . nusquam iam deōs ūllōs esse affirmābant. St. 46, p. 120, line 11.
. . . sē Agrippīnam esse . . . clāmat. St. 48, p. 158, line 14.
. . . praetōriānōs . . . obstrictōs esse respondit. St. 48, p. 159, lines 6–7.
. . . incolumem esse Agrippīnam vulgātum est. St. 48, p. 162, lines 6–7.
hunc fore suī fīnem . . . crēdiderat Agrippīna. St. 48, p. 163, lines 23–4.

The second part of example 1 in paragraph 4 might be compared with *medicī . . . dēspērābant*; guide pupils to see that this would be a comment by the narrator and not part of the slave's announcement. The teacher could devise similar pairs of examples for comparison, e.g. *centuriō crēdēbat hostēs dēspērāre; ducem eōrum captum esse* (cf. *dux eōrum captus erat*).

Further examples in which an indirect statement follows either another indirect statement or an indirect command or a phrase such as *cōnsilium prōposuit*:

omnibus . . . mortālibus . . . pereundum esse. St. 43, p. 54, line 24.
potius sē . . . neglegentiam . . . pūnitūrum esse. St. 43, p. 55, lines 8–9.
tē ipsam . . . quaesītūram, ac . . . habitūram esse. St. 43, p. 60, lines 10–11.
sē . . . libenter moritūram esse. St. 46, p. 116, lines 17–18.
nāvem posse compōnī . . . St. 48, p. 153, line 11.
. . . ōrāre ut Nerō . . .; sibi . . . quiēte opus esse. St. 48, p. 158, lines 26–7.

Uses of the participle (p. 211). Examples of the participle used substantivally (cf. sentence 3 in pupil's text):

spectantibus St. 41, p. 18, line 8.
lūgentis . . . mortuī . . . lūgentem St. 43, p. 53, lines 18, 22, 23.
sepultī St. 44, p. 81, line 16.
amantī St. 45, p. 98, line 3. *amantem* St. 45, p. 99, line 7.
fugientium St. 46, p. 120, line 4.
sequentem . . . euntem St. 47, p. 138, lines 3, 17.
irrumpentium St. 48, p. 162, line 11.

The class might be asked to explain why the ablative absolute is used in sentence 6 but not in sentence 5 (or why sentence 5 does not contain a word for 'it'). For further examples of the perfect passive participle used in the accusative, see Appendix B.

Conditional sentences (pp. 212–13). The class might use sentence 3 in paragraph 4 to practise the two ways of translating *nisi* given in paragraph 3. Which way do they think would be more appropriate for translating sentence 4?

Conditional sentences using the pluperfect subjunctive have appeared several times in the pupil's text; they have been discussed in a language note in Stage 46 and practised in a manipulation exercise in Stage 47. One example of a conditional sentence with the present subjunctive occurred in Stage 45 (p. 98, line 2) and two with the imperfect subjunctive in Stage 42 (p. 32, line 10, and p. 37, III, line 2). Further examples with the present and imperfect subjunctive are included here in paragraphs 5 and 6 for those teachers who wish their class to practise the full range of tenses used in conditional sentences; but they are fairly difficult for most pupils, many of whom will be relatively unpractised in the different English forms required ('If I were sitting here . . .', 'If you were to say that . . .', or 'If you did that . . .' referring to the future), and many teachers will prefer to concentrate on the pluperfect subjunctive, postponing further discussion of present and imperfect until pupils have met more examples in their reading. It is, however, worth emphasising to pupils the general point that if the verbs in a conditional sentence are subjunctive, the English translation of the main verb will normally contain 'would' or 'should'.

Gerund and gerundive (pp. 214–15). Pupils could be asked what nouns or pronouns the gerundives in paragraph 2 are agreeing with; are they singular or plural, and what is their gender? (For example, how can we tell that *nōs* in sentence 1 is masculine?) These examples can then be compared with those in paragraph 1, and the point can be elicited that the gerund, unlike the gerundives in paragraph 2, has no noun agreeing with it.

When discussing paragraph 3, prompt the pupils to recall examples of gerundives of obligation that have passed into English, such as Amanda, referendum, memorandum, *(quod erat) demonstrandum* and other examples quoted in Unit IIIB Handbook, p. 157. If the class asks anxiously 'How can we tell whether a gerundive means "ought" or not?' compare pairs of examples of the different types of gerundive, e.g. *latrō interficiendus est* and *centuriō gladium dēstrīnxit ad latrōnem interficiendum*, and invite pupils to say what differences they notice between the two sentences. Confirm that the gerundive of obligation is usually used in the nominative and accompanied by part of *esse*, whereas other gerundives are normally used in the accusative, genitive, dative or ablative, and are unaccompanied by any part of *esse*. (At this stage, discussion of exceptions to these generalisations is unlikely to be very profitable. If pupils ask, the only examples they have met of gerundives of obligation in a case other than nominative are *repetenda*, Stage 44, p. 78, line 3, and some examples in indirect statement.)

Hitherto, the vast majority of the gerundives met by the pupils (except those of obligation) have been in the accusative with *ad*, but the teacher might quote some simple examples in other cases, such as *servus artem cibī coquendī didicit* or *Nerō amīcōs dē mātre interficiendā cōnsuluit* to demonstrate that the context normally makes the significance of the gerundive clear.

Longer sentences (pp. 216–17). Encourage comment on the examples in paragraph 1. For instance, pupils may notice, with or without a little prompting, that main clauses and subordinate clauses each contain a verb. The final point in the paragraph can be demonstrated by getting pupils to write down subordinate clauses in English ('because I was tired', 'which I saw yesterday', etc.) for other pupils to turn into complete sentences by adding main clauses.

After paragraphs 1–3 have been read, the teacher might write up the first examples from paragraphs 1 and 4 on the blackboard and invite the class to compare them, eliciting that one is a direct statement, the other indirect, and that in the latter the verb in the subordinate clause is subjunctive; the class could then return to page 217 of the pupil's text for further study of paragraphs 4 and 5.

The main point to emphasise is the use of the subjunctive. (Guide the class to see that in sentence 1 of paragraph 5 the relative clause is part of what the slave said, whereas *quās ille senex vēndit* would be an incidental comment by the narrator.) Some observant pupils, on comparing the second examples in paragraphs 1 and 4, may note that the verb in the indirect statement has not only become subjunctive but also changed its tense; confirm that this happens regularly after a past verb of speaking, etc., and point out that the same change of tense occurs in the English translation.

Further examples:

affirmāvērunt nūllum perīculum īnstāre quod Salvius vir magnae auctōritātis esset. St. 40, p. 106, lines 6–7.
dīxit . . . imāginem . . . quae aulam rēgis Cogidubnī ōrnāvisset ā Salviō . . . vēnditam esse. St. 40, p. 108, lines 10–12.
affirmāvit mē, quod iuvenis essem, . . . posse. St. 46, p. 116, line 17.
sē, quae . . . gravārētur, . . . moritūram esse. St. 46, p. 116, lines 17–18.

Vocabulary

Remind the pupils that although the kind of checking described and practised in paragraphs 3 and 4 of the Notes is sometimes advisable, it is often clear from the whole sentence whether a particular word is part of a deponent verb or not. For example, *hortābātur* in sentence 1 must be from a deponent verb and have an active meaning; for if it were a passive form of an ordinary verb, it would mean 'he was being urged on', and it would be impossible to fit the accusative *mīlitēs* into the sentence.

The teacher might also demonstrate to the class how to use this part of the Language Information section to check the conjugation of a verb in order to identify the following forms:

-ēs . . . -ent, -ēris . . . -entur, which may be present tense of a 2nd conjugation verb, or future of 3rd or 4th conjugation, or present subjunctive of 1st conjugation
(Examples: *habēmus*, *mittēmus*, *laudēmus*; *salūtentur*, *dūcentur*, *monentur*)

-as . . . -ant, -āris . . . -antur, which may be present indicative of a 1st conjugation verb, or present subjunctive of 2nd, 3rd or 4th conjugation
(Examples: *audiās*, *necās*; *vocāminī*, *regāminī*; *precātur*, *sequātur*)

-am, *-ar*, which may be present subjunctive of a 2nd conjugation verb,

or present subjunctive/future indicative (indistinguishable) of 3rd or 4th conjugation

(Examples: *iubeam*, *dormiam*)

Care should be taken not to overdo work of this kind and to give generous help if pupils show signs of confusion. Emphasise that the context of a sentence will often provide plenty of clues to the meaning of a verb form.

Linguistic synopsis of Unit IVB

For general comments, see Unit I Handbook, p. 84. LI = Language Information section.

Stage	*Linguistic feature*	*Place of language note, etc.*
41	gerund with *ad*	41, LI
	fīō	41, LI
	present subjunctive passive (including deponent)	41, LI
	conditional clauses	42
	locative	LI
42	conditional clauses (met from Stage 41)	42, LI
	verse word order: NOUN + ADJECTIVE phrases interlaced with each other (met from Stage 39)	42
	imperfect subjunctive deponent (one example)	43
	dative of disadvantage	45
	indirect statement with *negō*	LI
	conditional clauses with imperfect subjunctive (two examples)	LI
43	imperfect subjunctive passive (including deponent from Stage 42)	43, LI
	genitive and ablative of gerund	43, LI
	position of verb of speaking, asking, etc., with indirect statement and question	43, LI
	conditional clauses with pluperfect subjunctive (two examples)	46
	indirect statement with verb of speaking, etc. omitted	LI

44	historic present (from Stage 39)	44, LI
	3rd person plural perfect in *-ēre* (from Stage 36)	44, LI
	omission of word from one of two clauses	44
	ablative meaning 'in' without preposition	47
45	jussive subjunctive	45, LI
	relative clauses with antecedent deferred or omitted	45, LI
	dative of disadvantage (from Stage 42) and advantage	45, LI
	conditional clauses with present subjunctive (one example)	LI
46	pluperfect subjunctive passive (including deponent)	46, LI
	conditional clauses with pluperfect subjunctive (from Stage 43)	46, LI
	omission of forms of *esse*	46, LI
	historic infinitive	48
	subordinate clauses in indirect statement	LI
47	ablative meaning 'in' or 'from' without preposition (cf. Stage 44)	47, LI
	plural for singular	47, LI
	quibus est possessive	LI
48	perfect subjunctive passive (including deponent)	48, LI
	historic infinitive (from Stage 46)	48
	direct and indirect deliberative question (from Stage 38)	48

The following terms are used in Unit IVB. Numerals indicate the stage in which each is introduced.

gerund	41	(direct) deliberative question	48
conditional clause	42	indirect deliberative question	48
conditional sentence	42	historic infinitive	48
verb of speaking, asking, etc.	43	ablative of comparison	LI
historic present	44	locative	LI
jussive subjunctive	45	gerundive of obligation	LI
dative of advantage	45	main clause	LI
dative of disadvantage	45	subordinate clause	LI

Appendix A: Attainment test

For notes on the purpose of the attainment tests, and suggestions for their use, see Unit I Handbook, p. 88. The words in heavy print have not occurred in the stage checklists. A few words not in the checklists are not in heavy print, if their meaning is obvious or if they have occurred frequently or prominently in recent stages.

Test 14

This should be worked after the class have finished Stage 48. Parts I and II could be taken either in a single period or in two consecutive ones, with another period spent on Part III.

Part I: introduction

This should be translated orally and informally with the class.

incendium
Nerōne imperātōre, incendium maximum Rōmae accidit.
initium in eā parte Circī Maximī ortum est quae Palātīnō
Caeliōque montibus **adiacet**; deinde flammae per tabernās
proximās, in quibus multum inerat **mercimōnium**, celerrimē
sunt sparsae. 5

Part II: comprehension test

cīvēs, quī in illā regiōne urbis habitābant, prīmō flammās
exstinguere cōnātī sunt; amīcīs et familiīs **hamās** trādidērunt
quibus aquam ferrent. tandem, dē domibus dēspērantēs,
salūtem fugiendō petere cōnstituērunt. sed tanta erat
multitūdō ut paucī ad loca tūta per viās angustās pervenīre 10
possent. multī, quia vel fessī vel ignārī viārum erant, flammīs
circumventī periērunt. praetereā, turba fugientium eōs
impediēbat quī aquam ferēbant. nōnnūllī quidem, omnī spē
effugiendī **omissā**, in domibus suīs mortem exspectāre
māluērunt. 15

illō tempore, Nerō ab urbe aberat; nam Antium ierat ad
diem fēstum celebrandum. nūntiātō tamen incendiō, Rōmam
profectus est. celerrimē equitandō, iter duābus hōrīs cōnfēcit.

simulatque advēnit, illīs cīvibus, quōrum domūs dēlētae
erant, hortōs suōs patefēcit, ubi aedificia **subitāria** exstruī 20
iussit. hīs tamen beneficiīs favōrem populī sibi haudquāquam
conciliāvit; rūmor enim **vagābātur** Nerōnem, cum flammae
urbem cōnsūmerent, montem proximum ascendisse unde
Rōmam ardentem spectāret, atque versūs aliquōs dē **excidiō**
Trōiae compositōs cantāvisse. **reminīscēbantur** quoque cīvēs 25
Nerōnem mātrem suam occīdisse, deōsque contempsisse. 'sī
imperātor noster homō minus **impius** fuisset', sibi inquiunt,
'deī hanc clādem nōbīs nōn mīsissent.'

		Marks
1	What was the citizens' first reaction to the outbreak of fire?	1
2	How did they get their friends and households to help them?	2
3	What decision did they eventually take (lines 8–9)?	1
4	'sed tanta . . . periērunt' (lines 9–12). Find three reasons why many people failed to escape.	3
5	What further difficulty was caused by those who were running away?	2
6	What did some people prefer to do? Why did they not behave like the others?	3
7	Why was Nero away from Rome when the fire broke out?	2
8	How long did his journey back to Rome take, and why?	2
9	What action did he then take, and for whose benefit (lines 19–20)?	3
10	What order did he give?	2
11	How grateful were the citizens for these kind actions (lines 21–2)?	1
12	According to the rumour, where had Nero gone when the fire was at its height, and for what purpose? What else was he believed to have done?	4
13	Read lines 25–8 ('reminīscēbantur . . . mīsissent.'). What explanation occurred to the citizens for the disaster they had suffered?	2
14	What previous actions of Nero made this explanation seem likely to them?	2
		30

Part III: written translation

per quīnque diēs incendium saeviēbat. flammīs sextō diē
exstīnctīs, **damnum aestimārī** poterat. cognōvērunt
magistrātūs ex quattuordecim urbis regiōnibus quattuor 30

tantum **integrās** manēre; trēs omnīnō dēlētās esse; in cēterīs superesse aedificia pauca. nisi cīvēs mīlitēsque strēnuissimē labōrāvissent ad incendium exstinguendum, tōta urbs flammīs cōnsūmpta esset.

deinde novī rūmōrēs per urbem **serpēbant**; multī iam crēdēbant Nerōnem ipsum Rōmam incendī iussisse, ut urbs secunda, priōre splendidior, exstruerētur. quibus rūmōribus audītīs, Nerō in hominēs quōsdam, quī Chrīstiānī appellābantur, culpam trānsferre cōnātus est. quī, ā mīlitibus Nerōnis comprehēnsī, crūdēliter interfectī sunt. Nerō enim imperāvit ut aliī in amphitheātrō contrā leōnēs pugnāre cōgerentur, aliī, vestīmenta **picea** gerentēs et **pālīs affīxī**, nocte ad lūcem praebendam in hortīs pūblicīs incenderentur. quō spectāculō vīsō, multī cīvēs, quamquam Chrīstiānī eīs erant odiō, **misericordiā** movēbantur. 35 40 45

Teachers may like to note how pupils are coping with the following features in particular:

is quī, etc.: *eōs . . . quī* (lines 12–13); *illīs cīvibus quōrum . . .* (19).
gerund: *fugiendō* (9); *effugiendī* (14); *equitandō* (18).
gerundive with *ad*: *ad diem fēstum celebrandum* (16–17); *ad incendium exstinguendum* (33); *ad lūcem praebendam* (43).
indirect statement: *Nerōnem . . . cantāvisse* (22–5); *Nerōnem . . . contempsisse* (26); *ex . . . pauca* (30–2); *Nerōnem . . . iussisse* (36).
conditional clauses with pluperfect subjunctive: *sī . . . mīsissent* (26–8); *nisi . . . cōnsūmpta esset* (32–4).
present passive infinitive: *aestimārī* (29); *incendī* (36).
pluperfect subjunctive passive: *cōnsūmpta esset* (34).
substantival participle: *fugientium* (12).
ablative of comparison: *priōre* (37).
connecting relative: *quibus* (37); *quī* (39); *quō* (44).
imperfect subjunctive passive: *cōgerentur* (42); *incenderentur* (43).
vocabulary: *haudquāquam* (21); *tantum* (31); *quīdam* (38).

The later reading passages in Dunlop, and the earlier ones in Dale, may also be useful during the reading of Unit IVB when the teacher wishes to assess pupils' progress and give the class practice in working unaided. Several passages in both Dunlop and Dale systematically practise particular syntactic points.

Appendix B: Classified examples of some linguistic features

For suggestions on the use of these examples, see the introduction to the Language Information section on p. 127 above. Most of the examples are taken from the text of Unit IVB; a few have been made up.

1 Perfect passive participle in accusative

repertōs St. 41, p. 12, line 2.
correptum St. 42, p. 30, line 13.
dētractum St. 43, p. 55, line 3.
dētracta St. 43, p. 59, line 8.
cēlātum St. 43, p. 59, line 14.
compositās St. 44, p. 74, line 2.
victam St. 47, p. 130, line 16.
convocātōs St. 48, p. 152, line 3.

Encourage the pupils not only to analyse the participial phrase and identify the noun to which the participle refers but also to produce natural and idiomatic translations.

2 Predicative and appositional use of noun or adjective

voluntāriī St. 41, p. 13, line 3.
vicāriī St. 41, p. 13, line 4.
superior St. 42, p. 30, line 2.
īnferior St. 42, p. 30, line 3.
morbum St. 42, p. 32, line 7.
candidī St. 45, p. 102, line 3.
attonitī St. 46, p. 120, line 18.
signum St. 47, p. 129, line 6.
rēctor . . . magister St. 47, p. 132, line 4.
interior St. 47, p. 134, line 3.

3 Variations of word order

(a) verb + accusative + nominative
īnstrūxit mīlitēs centuriō.
īnspiciēbant victimam haruspicēs.
involvēre diem nimbī. St. 42, p. 42, line 7.
irrūpit cubiculum meum māter. St. 46, p. 115, lines 5–6.

(b) accusative + verb + nominative
hastās coniēcērunt barbarī.
eōs spectābat dominus.
altum tenuēre ratēs. St. 42, p. 42, line 1.
eum ... audiit ... omnis Nēreidum ... chorus. St. 47, p. 138, lines 15–16.

(c) accusative + nominative + verb
culpam mīlitēs in servōs ... trānsferre poterunt. St. 41, p. 6, lines 7–8.
quīntum ... diem mātrōna sine cibō agēbat. St. 43, p. 53, line 11.
amantem iniūria tālis cōgit amāre magis. St. 45, p. 99, lines 7–8.
illum ... Teucrī ... rīsēre. St. 47, p. 132, line 9.
hōs successus alit. St. 47, p. 138, line 7.

(d) dative + nominative + verb
āctōribus spectātōrēs plausērunt.
captīvo rēx pepercit.
sī precibus nostrīs fortūna fāvisset ... St. 43, p. 60, line 3.

(e) verb + nominative (very common; the following are a few of the examples to be found in Unit IVB)
inveniuntur mēnsōrēs. St. 41, p. 5, lines 8–9.
manent ... paucissimī arcūs. St. 41, p. 10, line 8.
dēcurrit ... liquor. St. 42, p. 30, line 8.
... docentur equī. St. 42, p. 40, line 4.
ingeminant ... ignēs. St. 42, p. 42, line 8.
tābuerant cērae. St. 44, p. 81, line 8.
fulsēre ... sōlēs. St. 45, p. 102, line 3.
iam dēcidēbat cinis. St. 46, p. 120, line 1.
effugit ... Gyās. St. 47, p. 130, lines 11–12.
exarsit ... dolor. St. 47, p. 132, line 1.
cōnsurgunt nautae. St. 47, p. 134, line 5.
metuēbat Nerō ... St. 48, p. 152, line 8.
placuit Nerōnī calliditās. St. 48, p. 154, line 1.
stābat prope vīllam nāvis. St. 48, p. 154, line 5.

(f) separation of noun and adjective (very common, especially in verse; many examples are highlighted in the pupil's text by underlining, and some of the remainder are listed below)
mollī ... aquā St. 42, p. 40, line 8.
flāvam ... cēram St. 44, p. 74, line 6.
ignōtās ... ālās St. 44, p. 76, line 7.
audācī ... volātū St. 44, p. 80, line 4.
nūdōs ... lacertōs St. 44, p. 81, line 8.
tenuis ... flamma St. 45, p. 92, lines 9–10.

rapidā . . . aquā St. 45, p. 98, line 4.
meum . . . amōrem St. 45, p. 105, line 21.
viridem . . . mētam St. 47, p. 129, line 5.
longā . . . carīnā St. 47, p. 130, line 18.
salsōs . . . flūctūs St. 47, p. 132, line 10.
spatiō . . . inīquō St. 47, p. 134, line 3.
frāctōs . . . rēmōs St. 47, p. 134, line 7.
scopulō . . . altō St. 47, p. 137, line 3.
candentem . . . taurum St. 47, p. 138, line 12.
portū . . . altō St. 47, p. 138, line 19.

Appendix C: Summary of changes from the first edition of the course

Unit IVB corresponds to Units IV and V of the first edition. The following changes have been made:

1 The material from Catullus, Ovid, Pliny and Tacitus which previously appeared in the pamphlets 'Bithynia', 'odi et amo', 'miser Catulle', 'mira arte' and 'Nero et Agrippina' has been retained with substantial additions and omissions.

2 The material which previously appeared in the pamphlets 'domi', 'vivite mortales moneo', 'mors omnibus instat' and 'Dido et Aeneas' has been replaced by new material selected or adapted from Catullus, Martial, Ovid, Petronius, Phaedrus, Pliny, the 'laudatio Turiae' inscription and Virgil.

3 The total length of the **reading material** has been reduced by about 320 lines. It has been arranged in a series of numbered Stages, as in earlier Units, and is selected and adapted in accordance with the linguistic scheme, which systematically develops the language of earlier Units in a gradual transition to original Latin.

4 New **vocabulary** has been reduced by about 250 words.

5 **Language notes** have been added, dealing with the gerund, conditional clauses, verse word order, the subjunctive passive and other linguistic points.

6 Many new **illustrations**, both photographs and line drawings, have been provided. Captioned drawings have been used with the reading material to highlight new linguistic features.

7 **Background material**, **manipulation exercises** and **vocabulary checklists** have been added.

8 The pamphlet 'information about the language: Units IV and V' has been replaced by a new **Language Information section**, printed at the end of the Unit.

9 The **Handbook** material in Units IV and V of the first edition has been extensively rewritten, and an attainment test added.

Appendix D: Words and phrases in checklists of Units I–IVB

Words and phrases in the Unit IVB checklists are printed in heavy type.

ā, ab (= 'by') (21)
ā, ab (='from') (17)
abesse (6)
abīre (10)
ac (28)
accidere (25)
accipere (10)
accūsāre (26)
ācriter (33)
ad (3)
addere (32)
adeō (27)
adeptus (22)
adesse (5)
adhūc (30)
adipīscī (34)
adīre (20)
aditus (27)
adiuvāre (21)
adloquī (42)
administrāre (23)
adstāre (24)
advenīre (13)
adventus (27)
adversus (adj.) (32)
adversus (prep.) (40)
aedificāre (16)
aedificium (13)
aeger (13)
aequō animō (32)
aequor (47)
aequus (32)
aestās (45)
afficere (30)
affirmāre (40)
ager (35)
agere (4)
aggredī (43)
agitāre (8)
agmen (15)
agnōscere (9)
agricola (5)
aliī . . . aliī (29)
aliquandō (29)
aliquid (18)
aliquis (25)
alius (15)
alter (13)
altus (31)
amāre (19)
ambō (30)
ambulāre (5)
amīcitia (40)
amīcus (2)
āmittere (12)
amor (22)
amplectī (34)
amplexus (29)
amplissimus (37)
amplius (37)
an (35)
ancilla (2)
angustus (31)
animadvertere (36)
animus (17)
annus (21)
ante (31)
anteā (27)
antīquus (14)
ānulus (4)
aperīre (25)
appārēre (27)
appellāre (32)
appropinquāre (17)
aptus (38)
apud (14)
aqua (15)
āra (17)
arbor (39)
arcessere (20)
ardēre (27)
argenteus (14)
arma (36)
arrogantia (28)
ars (20)
ascendere (21)
aspicere (44)
at (33)
atque (28)
ātrium (1)
attonitus (14)
auctor (34)
auctōritās (24)
audācia (29)
audāx (24)
audēre (18)
audīre (5)
auferre (26)
augēre (40)
aula (14)
aureus (22)
auris (20)
aurum (37)
aut (39)
autem (25)
auxiliō esse (40)
auxilium (16)
avārus (6)
avidē (22)
avis (32)

barbarus (21)
bellum (26)
bellum gerere (26)
bene (17)
beneficium (28)
benignus (17)
bibere (3)
bona (43)
bonus (16)
bracchium (38)
brevis (33)

cadere (39)
caecus (42)
caedere (19)
caedēs (48)
caelum (22)
callidus (10)

campus (39)
candidus (45)
canis (1)
cantāre (13)
capere (10)
capillī (39)
captīvus (25)
caput (18)
carcer (24)
carēre (47)
carmen (29)
cārus (19)
castīgāre (19)
castra (25)
cāsus (32)
catēna (31)
causa (36)
cautē (19)
cavēre (35)
cēdere (23)
cēlāre (21)
celebrāre (9)
celeriter (9)
cēna (2)
cēnāre (7)
centum (28, 33, 39 & 48)
centuriō (7)
cēra (4)
certāmen (27)
certāre (33)
certus (38)
cēterī (13)
cibus (2)
cinis (12)
circum (21)
circumspectāre (3)
circumvenīre (29)
cīvis (9)
clādēs (46)
clam (38)
clāmāre (3)
clāmor (5)
clārus (23)
claudere (15)
cliēns (31)
coepisse (18)
cōgere (25)
cōgitāre (19)
cognōscere (18)
cohors (26)
colligere (26)
collocāre (20)
colloquium (24)
comes (27)
comitārī (34)
commemorāre (23)
commendāre (38)
commodus (15)
commōtus (26)
comparāre (19)
complēre (12)
complūrēs (37)
compōnere (32)
comprehendere (24)
cōnārī (34)
cōnātus (32)
condūcere (32)
cōnfectus (38)
cōnficere (19)
cōnfīdere (21)
conicere (33)
coniungere (44)
coniunx (37)
coniūrāre (44)
coniūrātiō (13)
cōnscendere (24)
cōnsentīre (16)
cōnsilium (16)
cōnsistere (18)
cōnspicārī (34)
cōnspicātus (23)
cōnspicere (7)
cōnstat (37)
cōnstituere (28)
cōnsul (40)
cōnsulātus (34)
cōnsulere (30)
cōnsūmere (8)
contemnere (43)
contendere (5)
contentus (10)
contrā (33)
convenīre (11)
convertere (32)
cōpiae (38)
coquere (4)
coquus (1)
corōna (29)
corpus (28)
cotīdiē (14)
crās (33)
creāre (30)
crēdere (11)
crēscere (44)
crīmen (40)
crūdēlis (20)
cubiculum (6)
culpa (45)
culpāre (37)
cum (= 'when') (24)
cum (= 'with') (7)
cupere (9)
cupīdō (44)
cūr (4)
cūra (23)
cūrae esse (35)
cūrāre (19)
cūria (40)
currere (5)
cursus (29)
custōdīre (12)
custōs (13)

damnāre (34)
dare (9)
dē (= 'about') (11)
dē (= 'down from') (19)
dea (18)
dēbēre (15)
decem (20, 28, 33, 39 & 48)
decēre (27)
dēcidere (13)
decimus (33, 39 & 48)
dēcipere (22)
decōrus (14)
dēfendere (19)
dēfessus (29)
dēicere (21)
deinde (16)
dēlectāre (16)
dēlēre (14)
dēmittere (30)
dēmōnstrāre (18)
dēmum (40)
dēnique (20)
dēnsus (12)
dēpōnere (25)
dērīdēre (16)
dēscendere (24)
dēserere (24)
dēsilīre (17)
dēsinere (25)
dēspērāre (17)

deus (14)
dextra (38)
dī immortālēs! (25)
dīcere (13)
dictāre (14)
diēs (9)
diēs nātālis (9)
difficilis (14)
dignitās (25)
dignus (37)
dīligenter (14)
dīligentia (25)
dīligere (28)
dīmittere (16)
dīrus (22)
discēdere (18)
discere (37)
discipulus (36)
discrīmen (39)
dissentīre (22)
diū (17)
dīversus (41)
dīves (30)
dīvitiae (30)
dīvus (37)
docēre (26)
doctus (20)
dolēre (28)
dolor (29)
domina (14)
dominus (2)
domus (20)
dōnāre (26)
dōnec (48)
dōnum (14)
dormīre (2)
dubitāre (37)
dubium (30)
ducentī (28, 33, 39 & 48)
dūcere (8)
dulcis (19)
dum (34)
duo (12, 20, 28, 33, 39 & 48)
duo mīlia (48)
duodecim (39 & 48)
duodēvīgintī (39 & 48)
dūrus (21)
dux (31)

ē, ex (4)
ecce! (3)
efferre (43)
efficere (21)
effigiēs (15)
effugere (16)
effundere (32)
ego (4)
ēgredī (34)
ēgressus (24)
ēheu! (4)
ēicere (33)
ēlātus (37)
ēligere (22)
emere (6)
ēmittere (9)
enim (23)
epistula (12)
eques (24)
equitāre (20)
equus (15)
ergō (39)
ēripere (38)
errāre (23)
esse (1)
et (3)
et . . . et (33)
etiam (15)
euge! (5)
eum (8)
ēvādere (48)
exanimātus (17)
excipere (33)
excitāre (13)
exclāmāre (10)
exemplum (37)
exercēre (9)
exercitus (37)
exilium (40)
exīre (3)
exīstimāre (40)
exitium (22)
explicāre (25)
exspectāre (3)
exstinguere (34)
exstruere (30)
extrā (25)
extrahere (21)
extrēmus (36)

faber (16)
fābula (5)
fābulam agere (5)
facere (7)
facile (8)
facilis (17)
facinus (26)
factum (41)
fallere (39)
falsus (26)
fāma (40)
familia (38)
familiāris (14)
favēre (11)
favor (31)
fax (27)
fēlīx (44)
fēmina (5)
ferōciter (6)
ferōx (8)
ferre (9)
ferrum (29)
fessus (13)
festīnāre (6)
fēstus (30)
fidēlis (14)
fidēs (26)
fīdus (43)
fierī (37)
fīlia (19)
fīlius (1)
fingere (40)
fīnis (36)
flamma (12)
flēre (45)
flōrēre (40)
flōs (16)
flūctus (47)
fluere (19)
flūmen (24)
fōns (21)
fortasse (18)
forte (19)
fortis (6)
fortiter (12)
fortūna (18)
forum (3)
fossa (15)
frāctus (15)
fragor (39)
frangere (18)
frāter (10)
fraus (31)
frūmentum (16)

frūstrā (12)
fuga (33)
fugere (12)
fulgēre (17)
fundere (22)
fundus (12)
fūr (6)
furēns (25)

gaudēre (27)
gaudium (34)
geminī (13)
gemitus (28)
gemma (17)
gēns (11)
genū (42)
genus (39)
gerere (23)
gladius (8)
glōria (41)
grātiās agere (19)
grātus (38)
gravis (21)
graviter (17)
gustāre (2)

habēre (4)
habitāre (8)
haerēre (17)
haesitāre (25)
haruspex (21)
hasta (17)
haud (34)
haudquāquam (31)
haurīre (13)
hercle! (10)
hērēs (28)
heri (7)
hic (8)
hīc (33)
hiems (20)
hinc (39)
hodiē (5)
homō (9)
honor (23)
honōrāre (15)
hōra (21)
horreum (13)
hortārī (34)
hortus (1)
hospes (9)
hostis (22)
hūc (17)
humī (24)

iacere (23)
iacēre (12)
iactāre (22)
iam (12)
iānua (3)
ibi (18)
īdem (31)
identidem (32)
ideō (35)
ideō . . . quod (35)
igitur (12)
ignārus (27)
ignāvus (8)
ignis (36)
ignōrāre (38)
ignōscere (32)
ille (9)
illūc (19)
immemor (25)
imminēre (34)
immortālis (25)
immōtus (23)
impedīre (15)
imperāre (27)
imperātor (16)
imperium (10)
impetus (17)
impōnere (34)
in (1)
in animō volvere (31)
inānis (37)
incēdere (29)
incendere (27)
incendium (41)
incēnsus (37)
incidere (12)
incipere (22)
incitāre (8)
incolumis (48)
inde (35)
indicium (34)
induere (23)
inesse (35)
īnfāns (6)
īnfēlīx (21)
īnferre (20)
īnfestus (24)
ingenium (23)
ingēns (7)
ingredī (34)
ingressus (22)
inicere (22)
inimīcus (10)
initium (37)
iniūria (30)
inopia (43)
inquit (4)
īnsānus (26)
īnsidiae (27)
īnspicere (9)
īnstruere (26)
īnsula (17)
intellegere (7)
intentē (6)
inter (16)
intereā (24)
interficere (13)
interim (40)
intrā (38)
intrāre (2)
invenīre (10)
invidēre (37)
invidia (40)
invītāre (11)
invītus (18)
iocus (27)
ipse (14)
īra (28)
īrātus (3)
īre (10)
irrumpere (20)
iste (14)
ita (16)
ita vērō (13)
itaque (17)
iter (19)
iterum (9)
iubēre (21)
iūdex (4)
iūdicāre (46)
iungere (38)
iussum (27)
iuvāre (39)
iuvenis (5)
iuxtā (43)

lābī (47)
labor (32)
labōrāre (1)
lacrima (22)
lacrimāre (7)

laedere (25)
laetus (2)
lapis (46)
latēre (25)
latrō (17)
latus (48)
lātus (20)
laudāre (2)
laus (47)
lavāre (14)
lectīca (34)
lectus (15)
lēgātus (26)
legere (11)
legiō (25)
lēniter (33)
lentē (15)
leō (3)
levis (40)
lēx (38)
libenter (18)
liber (10)
līberālis (11)
līberāre (20)
līberī (29)
lībertās (32)
lībertus (6)
licet (44)
līmen (38)
lingua (28)
littera (39)
litterae (39)
lītus (15)
locus (19)
locūtus (23)
longē (42)
longus (18)
loquī (34)
lūdere (41)
lūdus (30)
lūgēre (42)
lūmen (46)
lūna (20)
lūx (29)

magis (35)
magister (30)
magistrātus (43)
magnopere (24)
magnus (3)
male (35)
mālle (29)
malus (28)
mandāre (28)
mandātum (23)
māne (19)
manēre (9)
manus (= 'band') (27)
manus (= 'hand') (18)
mare (17)
marītus (14)
māter (1)
maximē (24)
maximus (17)
medicus (20)
meditārī (40)
medius (9)
melior (16)
meminisse (42)
mendāx (4)
mēns (38)
mēnsa (2)
mēnsis (39)
mentīrī (35)
mercātor (2)
merēre (41)
meritus (35)
metuere (48)
metus (28)
meus (5)
mīles (18)
mīlia (28)
mīlle (28 & 48)
minārī (40)
minimē! (11)
minimus (22)
minus (46)
mīrābilis (12)
mīrārī (36)
miser (15)
mittere (12)
modo (34)
modo . . . modo (45)
modus (23)
molestus (22)
mollis (42)
monēre (22)
mōns (12)
mora (47)
morārī (35)
morbus (21)
morī (34)
mors (20)
mortuus (7)
mōs (31)
movēre (33)
mox (9)
mulier (45)
multī (5)
multitūdō (17)
multō (28)
multus (5)
mūnus (48)
mūrus (11)
mūtāre (40)

nam (18)
nārrāre (7)
nāscī (34)
nātus (30)
nauta (15)
nāvigāre (16)
nāvis (3)
nē (36)
nē quid (48)
nē . . . quidem (32)
nē quis (48)
nec (42)
nec . . . nec (42)
necāre (7)
necesse (14)
negāre (43)
neglegēns (19)
neglegere (31)
negōtium (17)
negōtium agere (4)
nēmō (18)
neque (42)
neque . . . neque (24)
nescīre (25)
niger (36)
nihil (7)
nihilōminus (32)
nimis (30)
nimium (23)
nisi (33)
nōbilis (14)
nocēre (27)
nōlle (13)
nōmen (25)
nōn (3)
nōnāgintā (28, 33, 39 & 48)
nōndum (41)
nōngentī (48)
nōnne? (16)

nōnnūllī (21)
nōnus (33, 39 & 48)
nōs (10)
noster (11)
nōtus (9)
novem (20, 28, 33, 39 & 48)
nōvisse (19)
novus (13)
nox (18)
nūbere (38)
nūbēs (12)
nūllus (13)
num (26)
num? (14)
numerāre (13)
numerus (23)
numquam (17)
nunc (11)
nūntiāre (10)
nūntius (8)
nūper (21)
nusquam (24)

obicere (40)
oblivīscī (37)
obscūrus (29)
obstāre (18)
obstupefacere (33)
obviam īre (34)
occāsiō (37)
occīdere (28)
occupāre (26)
occupātus (21)
occurrere (27)
octāvus (33, 39 & 48)
octingentī (48)
octō (20, 28, 33, 39 & 48)
octōgintā (28, 33, 39 & 48)
oculus (20)
odiō esse (33)
ōdisse (29)
odium (37)
offendere (36)
offerre (9)
officium (35)
ōlim (6)
omnīnō (30)
omnis (7)
opēs (28)
oportet (26)
oppidum (21)
opprimere (32)
oppugnāre (24)
optāre (47)
optimē (12)
optimus (5)
opus (30)
opus est (41)
ōrāre (31)
ōrātiō (39)
orbis (45)
orbis terrārum (45)
ōrdō (13)
orīrī (38)
ōrnāre (23)
ōs (25)
ōsculum (27)
ostendere (9)
ōtiōsus (32)
ōtium (45)

paene (12)
pallēscere (30)
pallidus (28)
pār (36)
parāre (7)
parātus (16)
parcere (22)
parēns (20)
pārēre (23)
pars (18)
parum (47)
parvus (6)
passus (24)
patefacere (24)
pater (1)
patī (34)
patria (37)
patrōnus (31)
paucī (17)
paulātim (44)
paulīsper (9)
paulō (37)
paulum (46)
pauper (32)
pavor (30)
pāx (10)
pectus (48)
pecūnia (4)
peditēs (41)
pendēre (34)
per (6)
perdere (= 'destroy') (39)
perdere (= 'lose') (41)
perficere (29)
perfidia (26)
perfidus (24)
perīculōsus (18)
perīculum (19)
perīre (16)
perītus (21)
permōtus (32)
persuādēre (20)
perterritus (4)
perturbāre (37)
pervenīre (17)
pēs (8)
pessimus (20)
pestis (7)
petere (= 'attack') (5)
petere (= 'beg for') (18)
pietās (48)
placēre (11)
plaudere (5)
plaustrum (15)
plēnus (21)
plērīque (36)
plūrimī (19)
plūrimus (19)
plūs (21)
pōculum (7)
poena (25)
poenās dare (25)
poēta (4)
pollicērī (38)
pompa (19)
pondus (47)
pōnere (16)
pōns (24)
pontifex (38)
populus (29)
porta (8)
portāre (3)
portus (10)
poscere (19)
posse (13)
possidēre (43)
post (9)
posteā (18)
postquam (6)

postrēmō (18)
postrīdiē (16)
postulāre (8)
potēns (23)
potestās (33)
praebēre (26)
praeceps (27)
praecō (31)
praeesse (15)
praefectus (37)
praeficere (28)
praemium (27)
praesēns (36)
praesertim (36)
praesidium (18)
praestāre (30)
praeter (36)
praetereā (30)
praeterīre (31)
prāvus (23)
precārī (34)
precātus (22)
precēs (20)
premere (48)
pretiōsus (14)
pretium (21)
prīmus (11, 33, 39 & 48)
prīnceps (15)
prīncipia (26)
prior (15)
prius (29)
priusquam (34)
prō (18)
prō certō habēre (38)
probāre (40)
prōcēdere (7)
procul (34)
prōcumbere (18)
prōdere (40)
proelium (37)
profectus (32)
proficīscī (34)
prōgredī (34)
prōgressus (31)
prohibēre (38)
prōmittere (11)
prope (7)
propter (43)
prōvincia (26)
proximus (27)
prūdentia (22)

pūblicus (31)
puella (5)
puer (8)
pugna (11)
pugnāre (8)
pulcher (7)
pulsāre (6)
pūnīre (15)
putāre (35)

quadrāgintā (20, 28, 33, 39 & 48)
quadringentī (48)
quaerere (4)
quālis (27)
quam (= 'how') (14)
quam (= 'than') (10)
quamquam (14)
quandō? (35)
quantus (22)
quārē? (30)
quartus (33, 39 & 48)
quasi (34)
quattuor (20, 28, 33, 39 & 48)
quattuordecim (39 & 48)
-que (14)
querī (38)
quī (15)
quia (32)
quicquam (28)
quīcumque (42)
quīdam (32)
quidem (35)
quiēs (29)
quidquid (46)
quīndecim (39 & 48)
quīngentī (48)
quīnquāgintā (20, 28, 33 & 48)
quīnque (20, 28, 33, 39, & 48)
quīntus (33, 39 & 48)
quis? (4)
quisquam (45)
quisque (48)
quisquis (46)
quō? (18)
quō modō? (22)
quod (6)
quodcumque (42)

quondam (17)
quoniam (47)
quoque (2)
quot (26)
quotiēns (35)

rapere (11)
ratiōnēs (31)
rē vērā (32)
recipere (17)
recitāre (36)
rēctē (36)
recumbere (8)
recūsāre (18)
reddere (4)
redīre (15)
redūcere (29)
referre (26)
reficere (31)
regere (38)
rēgīna (33)
regiō (36)
rēgnum (26)
regredī (34)
regressus (23)
relēgāre (35)
relinquere (20)
reliquus (46)
remedium (20)
repente (43)
reperīre (42)
requīrere (46)
rēs (6)
rēs adversae (32)
resistere (18)
respicere (39)
respondēre (3)
retinēre (13)
revenīre (9)
revertī (34)
revocāre (37)
rēx (14)
rīdēre (3)
rīpa (24)
rogāre (7)
ruere (13)
rumpere (45)
rūrsus (25)
rūs (35)

sacer (18)
sacerdōs (15)

saepe (8)
saevīre (18)
saevus (26)
sagitta (47)
saltāre (16)
salūs (29)
salūtāre (2)
salvē! (3)
sānē (26)
sanguis (8)
sapiēns (21)
satis (4)
saxum (15)
scelestus (25)
scelus (29)
scindere (32)
scīre (23)
scrībere (6)
sē (13)
secāre (31)
secundus (11, 33, 39 & 48)
sēcūrus (37)
secūtus (32)
sed (4)
sēdecim (39 & 48)
sedēre (1)
sēdēs (30)
sella (14)
semper (10)
senātor (11)
senex (5)
sententia (10)
sentīre (12)
sepelīre (42)
septem (20, 28, 33, 39 & 48)
septendecim (39 & 48)
septimus (33, 39 & 48)
septingentī (48)
septuāgintā (28, 33, 39 & 48)
sepulcrum (30)
sequī (34)
serēnus (31)
sermō (20)
servāre (10)
servīre (29)
servus (1)
sescentī (48)
sevērus (33)
sex (20, 28, 33, 39 & 48)
sexāgintā (28, 33, 39 & 48)
sextus (33, 39 & 48)
sī (26)
sī quid (41)
sī quis (41)
sīc (28)
sīcut (20)
sīdus (42)
signum (4)
silentium (27)
silva (8)
similis (40)
simul (35)
simulac (16)
simulāre (39)
sine (17)
socius (40)
sōl (30)
solēre (17)
sollicitus (11)
sōlus (10)
solvere (28)
somnus (46)
sonitus (19)
sordidus (17)
soror (30)
sors (29)
spargere (39)
spatium (47)
speciēs (45)
spectāculum (8)
spectāre (5)
spērāre (31)
spernere (29)
spēs (28)
stāre (5)
statim (8)
statiō (25)
sternere (46)
stilus (39)
stola (19)
strēnuē (32)
strepitus (30)
studēre (44)
studium (39)
stultus (11)
suādēre (40)
suāvis (25)
suāviter (13)
sub (27)
subitō (6)
subvenīre (32)
summus (16)
sūmptuōsus (32)
superāre (6)
superbus (31)
superesse (16)
supplicium (35)
suprā (39)
surgere (3)
suscipere (21)
suspicārī (34)
suspicātus (28)
suus (9)

taberna (3)
tacēre (10)
tacitē (7)
tacitus (27)
taedēre (27)
tālis (23)
tam (20)
tamen (7)
tamquam (23)
tandem (12)
tangere (36)
tantum (24)
tantus (27)
tardus (22)
tēctum (= 'building') (46)
tēctum (= 'roof') (33)
tegere (45)
tellūs (44)
tempestās (30)
templum (12)
temptāre (20)
tempus (31)
tenebrae (34)
tenēre (15)
tenuis (45)
tergum (17)
terra (12)
terrēre (7)
tertius (11, 33, 39 & 48)
testāmentum (28)
testis (25)
timēre (12)
timor (30)

tollere (16)
tot (19)
tōtus (8)
trādere (9)
trahere (13)
trāns (38)
trānsīre (24)
trēcentī (48)
trēdecim (39 & 48)
trēs (12, 20, 28, 33, 39 & 48)
tribūnus (26)
trīgintā (20, 28, 33, 39 & 48)
trīstis (24)
tū (4)
tuba (8)
tum (6)
tum dēmum (40)
tumultus (40)
turba (5)
tūtus (22)
tuus (6)

ubi (= 'when') (14)
ubi (= 'where') (5)
ubīque (31)
ulcīscī (43)
ūllus (39)
ultimus (26)
ultiō (34)
ultrā (46)
umbra (7)
umerus (19)
umquam (23)
ūnā cum (44)
unda (15)
unde (21)
ūndecim (39 & 48)
ūndēvīgintī (39 & 48)
undique (29)
unguere (38)
ūnus (12, 20, 28, 33, 39 & 48)
urbs (5)
ut (= 'as') (28)
ut (= 'that') (26)
uterque (44)
ūtī (40)
ūtilis (11)
utrum (33)
utrum . . . an (35)
uxor (10)

vacuus (36)
valdē (7)
valē! (11)
validus (37)
vehementer (10)
vehere (31)
vel (34)
vel . . . vel (48)
velle (13)
velut (48)
vēnātiō (8)
vēndere (4)
venēnum (23)
venia (23)
venīre (5)
ventus (28)
verberāre (11)
verbum (22)
verērī (38)
vērō (38)
vertere (16)
vērum (24)
vērus (32)
vester (29)
vestīmenta (34)
vestis (38)
vetus (36)
vexāre (19)
via (1)
vīcīnus (35)
victor (15)
vidēre (3)
vidērī (40)
vīgintī (20, 28, 33, 39 & 48)
vīlis (41)
vīlla (3)
vincere (15)
vincīre (31)
vinculum (44)
vīnum (3)
vir (11)
vīrēs (47)
virgō (22)
virtūs (22)
vīs (48)
vīta (17)
vītāre (22)
vitium (41)
vituperāre (6)
vīvere (19)
vīvus (29)
vix (19)
vocāre (4)
volvere (31)
vōs (10)
vōx (19)
vulnerāre (13)
vulnus (20)
vultus (31)

Bibliography

Any bibliography for the range of authors and topics appearing in Unit IVB must necessarily be highly selective. The following list is restricted to the books and articles referred to in the main body of this Handbook.

Arias, P. E. *History of Greek Vase Painting* (Thames and Hudson 1962)

Austin, R. G. (ed.) *M. Tulli Ciceronis pro M. Caelio oratio* (Oxford U.P. 3rd edn 1960)

Balme, M. G. *Intellegenda* (Oxford U.P. (pbk) 1970)

Balme, M. G. *The Millionaire's Dinner Party* (Oxford U.P. (pbk) 1973)

Balme, M. G. and Greenstock, M. C. *Scrutanda* (Oxford U.P. (pbk) 1973)

Balme, M. G. and Warman, M. S. *Aestimanda* (Oxford U.P. (pbk) 1965)

Balsdon, J. P. V. D. *Life and Leisure in Ancient Rome* (Bodley Head 1969)

Balsdon, J. P. V. D. *Roman Women* (Bodley Head 2nd edn 1974)

Brett, S. (ed.) *The Faber Book of Useful Verse* (Faber 1981; pbk 1987)

Bruun, B. and Singer, A. *The Hamlyn Guide to Birds of Britain and Europe* (Hamlyn (pbk) 1970)

Cambridge School Classics Project *Greek Foundation Course Folder V* (Cambridge U.P. 1975)

Cambridge School Classics Project *The Roman World, Units I and II and Teacher's Handbook* (Cambridge U.P. 1978, 1979, 1980)

Camps, W. A. *An Introduction to Virgil's Aeneid* (Oxford U.P. (pbk) 1969)

Carcopino, J. *Daily life in Ancient Rome* (Penguin 1970)

Casson, L. *Travel in the Ancient World* (Allen and Unwin 1974)

Coleman, R. G. G. 'The study of language and the study of literature' in *Didaskalos* Vol. 2 no. 2 (1967)

Corbett, P. E. *The Roman Law of Marriage* (Oxford U.P. 1930 O.P.)

Crook, J. A. *Law and Life of Rome* (Thames and Hudson 1967)

Dale, C. M. *Latin Passages for Translation and Comprehension* (Cambridge Latin Texts, Cambridge U.P. (pbk) 1981)

Didaskalos (J.A.C.T., 31–34 Gordon Square, London WC1H 0PY)

Dilke, O. A. W. *The Ancient Romans: how they lived and worked* (David and Charles 1975 O.P.)

Dilke, O. A. W. *Greek and Roman Maps* (Thames and Hudson 1985)

Dilke, O. A. W. *The Roman Land Surveyors: an introduction to the agrimensores* (David and Charles 1971)

Drees, L. *Olympia: Gods, artists and athletes* (Pall Mall Press 1968)

Dunlop. P. *Short Latin Stories* (Cambridge U.P. (pbk) 1987)

Durry, M. *Eloge Funèbre d'une Matrone Romaine* (Budé 1950)

Feder, T. H. *Great Treasures of Pompeii and Herculaneum* (Abberville Press (pbk) 1978)

Fordyce, C. J. (ed.) *Catullus: a commentary* (Oxford U.P. 1961)

Furneaux, H. (ed.) *Tacitus: Annals* (2nd edn revised by H. F. Pelham and C. D. Fisher (Clarendon Press 1896–1907, repr. 1951–6)

Garnsey, P. and Saller, R. The Early Principate: Augustus to Trajan (*New surveys in the classics* No. 15, published by *Greece and Rome* in collaboration with J.A.C.T., Oxford U.P. (pbk) 1982)
Grant, M. (trans.) *Tacitus: the annals of imperial Rome* (Penguin (pbk) 1956, revised edn 1971)
Greece and Rome (Oxford U.P. for the Classical Association)
Greig, C. (ed.) *Experiments: nine essays on Catullus for teachers* (C.S.C.P. 1970) (available from Cambridge School Classics Project, 17 Panton Street, Cambridge CB2 1HL)
Griffin, M. T. *Nero: the end of a dynasty* (Batsford 1984)
Hamey, L. A. and Hamey, J. A. *Roman Engineers* (Introduction to the History of Mankind Series; Cambridge U.P. 1981)
Hammond, N. G. L. and Scullard, H. H. (eds.) *Oxford Classical Dictionary* (Oxford U.P. 2nd edn 1970)
Hardy, E. G. (ed.) *Pliny's Correspondence with Trajan* (Macmillan 1889)
Harris, H. A. *Sport in Greece and Rome* (Thames and Hudson 1972)
Harris, H. A. 'The Games in *Aeneid V*', in *Meminisse Iuvabit*, ed. F. Robertson (Bristol Classical Press 1988)
Hollis, A. S. (ed.) *Ovid: Ars Amatoria Book I* (Oxford U.P. 1977)
Hollis, A. S. (ed.) *Ovid: Metamorphoses Book VIII* (Oxford U.P. (pbk) 1970)
Horsfall, N. 'Some problems in the "Laudatio Turiae"' in *Bulletin of the Institute of Classical Studies*, Vol. 30 (1983)
James, M. R. *More Ghost Stories* (Edward Arnold 1911; Penguin (pbk) 1959)
Jones, P. V. *Selections from Tacitus: Histories I–III* (Cambridge Latin Texts, Cambridge U.P. (pbk) 1974)
Lefkowitz, M. R. 'Wives and husbands' in *Greece and Rome* Vol. 30, no. 1 (1983)
Lefkowitz, M. R. and Fant, M. B. *Women's Life in Greece and Rome* (Duckworth 1982)
Levens, R. G. C. (ed.) *A Book of Latin Letters* (Methuen 1930, 2nd edn. 1938)
Lewis, N. and Reinhold, M. *Roman Civilization: a sourcebook – Volume I: the republic; Volume II: the empire* (Harper Torchbooks, Harper and Row 1966)
Lyne, R. O. A. M. *The Latin Love Poets* (Oxford U.P. 1980)
Lyne, R. O. A. M. *Selections from Catullus: Handbook* (Cambridge Latin Texts, Cambridge U.P. (pbk) 1975)
Martindale, C. (ed.) *Ovid Renewed* (Cambridge U.P. 1988).
Massey, M. *Society in Imperial Rome* (Cambridge U.P. (pbk) 1982)
Millar, F. *The Emperor in the Roman World* (Duckworth 1977 O.P.)
Morford, M. P. O. 'Bruegel and the First *Georgic*' in *Greece and Rome* Vol. 13, no. 1 (1966)
Muir, J. V. 'The study of ancient literature' in *Didaskalos* Vol. 4, no. 3 (1974)
Omnibus and *Omnibus Omnibus* (J.A.C.T. 31–34 Gordon Square, London WC1H 0PY)
Page, T. E. (ed.) *The Aeneid of Virgil Books I–VI* (Macmillan 1894)
Paoli, U. E. *Rome, its People, Life and Customs* (Longmans 1963)
Quinn, K. (ed.) *Catullus: the poems* (Macmillan 1970; 2nd edn 1973)
Quinn, K. *Latin Explorations: critical studies in Roman literature* (Routledge and Kegan Paul 1963)
Richardson, J. *Roman Provincial Administration* (Inside the ancient world series: Macmillan Education (pbk) 1976; Bristol Classical Press (pbk) 1984)
Royal Academy Exhibition Catalogue *Pompeii A.D. 79* (Imperial Tobacco Ltd. 1976 O.P.)
Rudd, N. *Lines of Enquiry* (Cambridge U.P. 1976)

Sedgwick, W. M. (ed.) *The Cena Trimalchionis of Petronius* (Oxford U.P. 1925, 2nd edn 1950)
Sharwood Smith, J. E. *On Teaching Classics* (Students Library of Education; Routledge and Kegan Paul 1977)
Sherwin-White, A. N. *The Letters of Pliny: a historical and social commentary* (Oxford U.P.. 1966)
Sherwin-White, A. N. 'Pliny, the man and his letters' in *Greece and Rome* Vol. 16 no. 1 (1969)
Stace, C. and Jones, P. V. *Stilus artifex* (Cambridge U.P. (pbk) 1972)
Swaddling, J. *The Ancient Olympic Games* (British Museum Publications 1980)
Tennick, M. *Libellus: Selections from Horace, Martial, Ovid and Catullus: Handbook* (Cambridge Latin Texts, Cambridge U.P. (pbk) 1978)
Tingay, G. (ed.) *Comprehendite* (Longmans (pbk) 1973)
Tingay, G. (trans.) *Empire and Emperors: selections from Tacitus' Annals* (Cambridge U.P. (pbk) 1983)
Tingay, G. I. F. and Badcock, J. *These were the Romans* (Hulton 1972)
Toynbee, J. M. C. *Death and Burial in the Roman World* (Thames and Hudson 1971)
Verity, A. C. F. *Latin as Literature* (Macmillan (pbk) 1971)
Warde Fowler, W. *Social Life at Rome in the Age of Cicero* (Macmillan 1908)
Warmington, B. H. *Nero: reality and legend* (Chatto and Windus 1969)
Watson, G. R. *The Roman Soldier* (Thames and Hudson 1969)
Wilkinson, L. P. *Golden Latin Artistry* (Cambridge U.P. 1963 Bristol Classical Press 1982)
Williams, G. *Tradition and Originality in Roman Poetry* (Oxford U.P. 1968): abridged version *The Nature of Roman Poetry* (Oxford U.P. (pbk) 1970)
Williams, R. D. (ed.) *The Aeneid of Virgil Books 1–6* (Macmillan 1972)
Williams, R. D. (ed.) *P. Vergili Maronis Aeneidos Liber Quintus* (Oxford U.P. 1960)
Williams, R. D. (ed.) *P. Vergili Maronis Aeneidos Liber Tertius* (Oxford U.P. 1962)
Wiseman, T. P. *Catullus and his World* (Cambridge U.P. 1985)
Woodcock, E. C. *A New Latin Syntax* (Methuen 1959)
Woodcock, E. C. (ed.) *Tacitus: Annals Book XIV* (Methuen 1939)
Woodman, A. J. and West, D. (eds.) *Creative Imitation and Latin Literature* (Cambridge U.P. 1979)

Abbreviations

C.I.L. *Corpus Inscriptionum Latinarum* (Berlin, 1863–)
I.L.S. Dessau, H. *Inscriptiones Latinae Selectae* (Berlin, 1892–1916)